D0734023

Election Guide

by
MICHAEL MOORE

Downsize This
Stupid White Men
Dude, Where's My Country?
Will They Ever Trust Us Again?
The Fahrenheit 9/11 Reader

by MICHAEL MOORE and KATHLEEN GLYNN

Adventures in a TV Nation

MIKE'S
Election Guide
2008

by

MICHAEL MOORE

GRAND CENTRAL
PUBLISHING

NEW YORK   BOSTON

Cover image by Kai Regan/Corbis Outline. Back cover image by Cosmo Condina/TIB/Getty Images. Front flap images: Albo © fotolia.com (White House); © iStockphoto/Scott Anderson (fists); Catherine Ledner/Stone/Getty Images (donkey); © iStockphoto/Kathy Konkle (hands); Stacy Gold/Getty Images (elephant); Aberenyi © fotolia.com (sign); Mike Kemp/Getty Images (wedding cake). Back flap illustration by Mathilde Roussel.

Grand Central Publishing
Hachette Book Group
237 Park Avenue
New York, NY 10017

Visit our Web site at www.HachetteBookGroupUSA.com.
Visit Michael Moore at www.michaelmoore.com.

Printed in the United States of America

First Edition: August 2008

10 9 8 7 6 5 4 3 2 1

Grand Central Publishing is a division of Hachette Book Group, Inc. The Grand Central Publishing name and logo is a trademark of Hachette Book Group, Inc.

ISBN: 978-0-446-54627-0
LCCN: 2008932732

For Tony Benn, keep teaching us

In memory of Shirley Chisholm, my first vote
for President

Contents

CONTENTS

Introduction

Sam Graves of Missouri has a problem. He's a Republican *and* a member of Congress—and he's scared he may lose his seat in this year's election.

So he had an idea. He produced a TV ad where he doesn't mention that he is either a Republican OR a member of Congress! He believes that if the voters don't know either of these things about him, his chances of winning re-election are greatly improved.

How did we reach the point where a Republican from the South is frightened for his political life, afraid to even tell anyone he's a *Republican?* How did the word "Republican" replace "liberal" as the dirtiest word in politics?

Republican Congressman Tom Davis of Virginia sums up the problem this way: "The Republican brand is in the trash can. . . . If we were dog food, we'd be taken off the shelf."

After a disastrous war, the failure to catch bin Laden, millions of families losing their homes, the Katrina debacle, soaring gas prices feeding record oil company profits, and the largest national debt caused by the biggest spending and borrowing administration in American history, the country has had it with conservatives, right-wingers, and Republicans.

A thrilling election season is now upon us. Obama vs. McCain. One candidate has promised a presidency different from any other, one that will take us forward to embrace the hope of the twenty-first century.

The other candidate says he has no idea how to use a computer.

Welcome to *Mike's Election Guide,* my effort to make sense of this fall's race for the White House and Congress. Herein I answer the nation's most pressing questions: "Why Is John McCain So Angry?" "Do the Democrats Still Drink from a Sippy Cup and Sleep with the Light On?" "Can I Get into the Electoral College with Only a 2.0 GPA?" and "How Many Democrats Does It Take to Lose the Most Winnable Election in American History?"

It's a great year to be an American and a voter. Don't miss out on all the fun! And if you see Congressman Sam Graves of Missouri, give him a big shout-out: "Yo! REPUBLICAN!"

Michael Moore
July 17, 2008

*The difference between a democracy
and a dictatorship is that in a democracy
you vote first and take orders later; in a
dictatorship you don't have to waste
your time voting.*
—Charles Bukowski

*It's not the voting that's democracy,
it's the counting.*
—Tom Stoppard

1

"Ask Mike!"

Michael Moore answers questions on the street
from the American people about voting,
the 2008 presidential candidates,
and the issues facing the nation.

 *Seven years ago, in order to defeat the terrorists, I took the president's advice and went shopping. I have now rung up about $30,000 of debt on my credit cards, and the monthly payment on my adjustable rate mortgage has doubled. Have the terrorists won?*

Jules Crandall
Ft. Lauderdale, FL

ANSWER: No they haven't! You won. We won. We won because YOU went shopping. You, the American public, decided to let the terrorists have it. You went to the mall, I went to Best Buy, she hit Sam's Club, he went to the Hummer dealer, we all went to the bank to take out another mortgage, and everyone went to Disney-World *and* Disneyland! You shopped but you never dropped. You spent money you never had just like our brave President who spent money *he* didn't have. Now you, we, are in debt up to our eyelashes—and the terrorists are on the run.

Thanks to this newfound patriotism, Americans are now carrying more personal debt than at any time in our history. And because you, my fellow citizens, have been so willing to wage this war on terror, the credit card industry has seen profits rise from $27.4 billion in 2003 to $40.7 billion in 2007. And when you help American industries like this do well, that means *you* will do well. Because the next time you want a loan, *they* will have the money—*your* money—to lend back to you at a higher interest rate. That, my friends, is the beauty of Capitalism, and don't you ever forget it.

Ah, how great it feels to be winning the War on Terror, one strip mall at a time. Now, of course, no war is without its casualties. Unfortunately, during all this shopping, some people have gone under. Ten times as many bankruptcies are being filed today than during the Great Depression. Thirty million people have had their credit ratings ruined because they said "charge it" one too many times. And analysts predict that nearly 1.4 million homes will be foreclosed on in 2008 alone, a number unlike anything we've ever seen.

But what war doesn't have some collateral damage? So a million homes are snatched from hard-working Americans! THAT'S A SMALL PRICE TO PAY FOR FREEDOM!! If you want to be free from terrorist bombings, then you have to be willing to sacrifice, sacrifice, sacrifice! Sacrifice in order to defeat the enemy. And the enemy, my fellow Americans, is *not* the banks or MasterCard or Countrywide Financial. These companies are there to hand you the weapons you need to shop and buy. Unfortunately, not all soldiers in the fight against the terrorists know how to use their weapons. So we experience some fratricide. Stuff happens.

The important thing to remember here is that the terrorists have lost! OUR WAY OF LIFE has won! Yes, we will gladly strip naked at the airport if we have to. Yes, we will pay whatever the pump tells us to pay. Yes, you can listen in on my phone calls and read my private emails—hell, you can put a friggin' drill in my head and insert a thought-control chip on my frontal lobe—*just as long as you promise me that I will be safe and the terrorists will be defeated!* Wait, wait—is that a *100-inch* plasma screen TV I see over there in the window? I have to have it! I must protect America and kill more terrorists!!

Oh God, PLEASE . . . do you take Discover?

 *I'm doing my best to support the troops, but I just can't make up my mind: Should I buy a magnetic yellow ribbon for the back of my car, or should I simply fly a big American flag on the back of my Dodge Ram?*

Gladys Siple
Gatlinberg, TN

ANSWER: The big magnetic yellow ribbon with the imprint, "Support Our Troops," seems to be the popular choice. Although there are reports that on lesser-model Pontiacs the paint under the decals tends to bubble up and explode, most consumer Americans have been quite satisfied with them. It gives them a certain "patriotic" feeling. But even more, it allows the consumer American to do something that contributes significantly to the war effort—and nothing says "I Sacrificed!" like a big magnetic yellow ribbon on the back of your kick-ass SUV. The great thing about the magnetic sticker is that you don't have to permanently affix it to your nice new car. Why risk having to spend 20 bucks on some touch-up paint when you try to peel a real sticker from it? I mean, we love America and all, but 20 bucks is 20 bucks! Plus, with all the shopping we've done to defeat the terrorists, why make this whole sticker thing more trouble than it needs to be? I'm worn out just thinking about it. This patriotism business can be exhausting.

But we do it anyway. We do it because we know how good it makes our troops feel. Riding around in Baghdad, though they may not be fully protected with the armor we promised, at least the soldiers know that the America they are protecting is full of people on their way to the outlet mall with big yellow magnetized shout-outs next to their "Bite Me, I'm Yours" bumper stickers.

True, those with the yellow ribbons may oppose

paying the necessary taxes to fund the war and thus leave this debt for their grandchildren, but, heck, that's what grandchildren are for! And what quadriplegic vet doesn't get all misty-eyed when he looks out the window of his rat-infested room in the Walter Reed annex and sees a patriotic decal on the back of a Mercedes as it whizzes by on its way to Chevy Chase? It almost makes him want to re-up for Uncle Sam.

And while 400,000 vets wait in line for their disability claims from this war, they can at least take some comfort from the sea of ribbons flowing down the street. Sure, these vets are finding it hard to get a job—and thousands have come back to find their boss handing them a pink slip—but I'm sure many of them have a real sense of satisfaction knowing that the country they went to fight for has sent their jobs—including the job of making magnetic yellow ribbon decals—to China.

(Some vets have this suggestion for a 2009 version of the magnetic yellow ribbon: Have it read, "Support Our Troops" on one part of the ribbon and "Bring Them Home" on the other loop.)

 *If Iran has weapons of mass destruction, we should invade, right?*

Chuck Thompson
Greenwich, CT

ANSWER: Excuuuuuse me? Did you say the words, *"weapons of mass destruction"*? Take it back. I SAID TAKE IT BACK! I swear to God if I hear those words once more in my lifetime I'm going to punch somebody—and I'm a pacifist!

No greater lie was ever spoken to the American people than the lie that Iraq had weapons of mass destruction. That whopper bamboozled the country into war, a war that has brought death and injury to countless Iraqis and Americans. The vast majority of Americans initially supported the war and gave Bush an approval rating of 70 percent. That's how good of a lie it was.

So, here's my new policy: If any president or general or cable news pundit (are you listening, Wolfie?) says that "Country X has weapons of mass destruction," or is "building them," or is "thinking" of getting them, or is seen shopping at the Weapons of Mass Destruction Mall, I am going to say, plain and simple, "You are lying." My automatic assumption will be that not only am I being *lied* to, I'm being played big time so that Uncle Sam's hand can dig into my pocket and grab my money to pay off the latest batch of military contractors. I will not care how many speeches you make, how many cartoon drawings you show to the members of the United Nations, how much evidence you claim to have, or how many network reporters you've snookered. I will never, ever believe you.

On the outside chance there may be a legitimate threat to the United States, I will not be convinced of such threat until I actually see it with my own two eyes. So you can claim Iran has a "nuclear weapons program" all you want, but I will not believe it. For me to believe it, that Ahmadinejad guy would literally have to walk onto the stage of *American Idol* WITH THE VERY BOMB ITSELF IN HIS HANDS. Seriously, I will have to see the actual friggin' bomb, and THEN I want him to show me that he knows how to use it. (Of course, I don't want him to actually detonate the thing—at least not before they announce who's being cut this week from the show.)

Then and only then will I believe. But belief alone won't be enough to get me to do anything about it. Why should I? Nine other nations have the bomb and we've done nothing about *that*. We've let all the old Soviet missiles be scattered over who knows where, so why start to pretend that now we give a hoot?

A wise man (I.F. Stone) once said, "Every government is run by liars and nothing they say should be believed." Our lazy, useless, gullible media starts with the assumption the government is telling them *the truth*, and only when someone from outside the mainstream presents the evidence that a lie has been told do journalists get off their butts and investigate anything. After 8 years of a lying administration, you'd think the media would start with the assumption that their chain is getting jerked again.

Will I ever live to see the day when just one reporter at a White House press conference stands up and says the following: "Based on what you just said, Mr. President, we're going to assume you're a lying sack of sound bites. Would you please prove to us that what you said is not one more in a pile of lies we've had shoveled down our throats since you took office?"

Scott McClellan, Bush's former press secretary, could not believe how EASY it was to play the gullible press. Says McClellan: "If anything, the national press corps was probably *too* deferential to the White House and to the administration in regard to . . . the choice over whether to go to war in Iraq." The so-called, "'liberal media,'" he continued, "didn't live up to its reputation. If it had, the country would have been better served." And when asked whether the early critics of the Iraq war had been right, he responded, ". . . certainly on the buildup to the Iraqi war, we should have been listening some more to what they were saying, the American people should have been listening a little bit closer to some of what was being said." (Thanks, Scott. Now you say it. Wasn't that you booing me off the stage at the Oscars?)

So, no, Iran has no "nuclear program" or "weapons of mass destruction." That's the position we should all take and not budge from it until we see the mushroom cloud over Boise. Which, my fans in Boise, I can assure you, will be NEVER.

But didn't the Ayatollah have something do with 9/11?

Marilyn Wolcott
Midland, TX

ANSWER: God#@&*$@!!!! DIDN'T YOU HEAR WHAT I JUST SAID?! No!! Nobody had anything to do with 9/11 other than the bastards who killed all those people. Oh, and the very, very smart people who trained them and funded them. Who were *THEY?* Yeah, just a bunch of guys running around in a desert and living in a cave. Hey, I bet they have WEAPONS OF MASS DESTRUCTION, TOO! HAHAHA-HAHAA!! ME LOVE A GOOD LAUGH!!!

Okay, sorry. To answer your question, no, neither the Ayatollah nor the Iranians had anything to do with 9/11. No Iranians were on any of the planes. They were mostly Saudis (our friends who sell us the $150-a-barrel oil). But if Bush and McCain want us to go to war against Iran, then I fully expect to hear a 9/11 connection before this modest tome even hits the bookstores.

Remember the rule: THEY ARE ALWAYS LYING. MAKE THEM PROVE IT. How would they prove this one to satisfy me? I might accept independently-shot videotape of the Ayatollah at his travel agent's office buying 19 one-way first class tickets.

Let's leave Iran alone. The Iranian people want to be free and they will take care of their freedom by themselves. Just like we did in 1776. Just like the French did a few years later. Just like Nelson Mandela did. Just like the Sandinistas did. Just like the Spanish after Franco, and the Italians after Mussolini. Freedom isn't something you dispense like a Happy Meal. It has to be wanted by those being oppressed—and then they have to *fight* for it *themselves*. The French could (and did) lend us a hand in 1776, but they couldn't have just handed us our independence by ousting the British themselves. We had to be willing to risk our own lives in order for independence to work.

The Iraqis (as we see from their daily bombings and killings) clearly had it in them to wreak havoc on Saddam—but didn't. That was their choice. We went in there and overthrew him for them. *That* doesn't work. I'm sure they hated Saddam, but I'm also sure they liked going to the movies every week, having a drink every night, and I'm certain women liked wearing whatever they wanted and going wherever they damn well pleased.

Now most of the movie theaters have been shuttered and the bars driven underground. At least 40 Christian churches have been bombed or otherwise attacked, as has the only Jewish synagogue (Baghdad was one of only a few Arab capitals with a protected and open synagogue under Saddam). And since 2000 the life expectancy for an Iraqi male has dropped from 65 to 48 years. If the Iraqis had wanted Saddam gone, there's one thing history has proven—he would have been gone. People desperate to be free will stop at no lengths to be free.

But they don't get freedom from the barrel of a gun. All that brings is chaos, death, and $5-a-gallon gas.

Which presidential candidate do I want to have a beer with?

**Billy McKenzie
Zanesville, OH**

ANSWER: You are asking the wrong question. Because more people wanted to have a beer with

George W. Bush than John Kerry, they elected Bush president. But if the guy you want to go drinking with is not allowed to drive you home, should you even be near him? Let alone put him in charge of the Free World?

They say we Americans don't want to elect someone smarter than we are. They say we'd rather elect someone who is shitfaced and dumb. Why? So we can feel superior? So we can laugh at the idiot? Is that a nice thing to do? Do you think it was fair to put so much responsibility in W's hands when he clearly wasn't able to touch his nose with his finger or count backwards from 10? Looking back on it all now, it seems quite cruel of us, doesn't it?

The point of electing someone more sober and brilliant than we are is to make sure the country moves forward under a president who seeks to create a better world. Open up new worlds with new ideas. Find the cure for cancer. Make sure everyone has a home and a job and a great education. Make friends with our neighbors in the world. Believe that the earth is round and that it has an ozone layer as thin as a piece of dental floss.

When Hillary Clinton said that she didn't realize that Bush was lying to her about the weapons of mass destruction, she was essentially saying, "I'm dumber than the dumb guy who is trying to get one over on me. And therefore that makes me not as smart as the 100 million Americans who were against the war from the beginning, the third of the country who *knew* Bush was lying." It simply doesn't work if 100 million Americans are smarter than the President.

Hillary then went campaigning around the country, pounding back brewskies in bars and honkytonks in the hopes of getting the "Who Would I Like to Have a Beer With" vote.

John McCain, too, is going for the same "Real Men Drink Bud and Fight Wars for 100 Years" crowd. His entire M.O. is that folksy, gee whiz, "Listen, my friends," demeanor. It's "my friends" this and "my friends" that. McCain proposed that he and Obama hold a series of down-home town hall meetings so that he could continue his have-a-beer-with-me persona. The idea of a real debate with tough questions where he would have to give hard facts is simply something he can't do when he's buying everyone in the town hall a round.

Fortunately, it seems that the American people (or at least those voting in the Democratic primaries in 2008) have wised up. After having the crap kicked out of the country for eight years by a dry drunk at the wheel, the last thing anyone wants is someone who can drink them under the table.

Fortunately, no one this year is asking, "Who do I want to have a beer with?" Rather, the new question is, "Who Do I Want to Have Sex With?" Now isn't that a better question? And isn't the answer obvious?

I cannot wait, 'til 2008
—Baby you're the best candidate—
I like it when you get hard
—On Hillary in debate—
Why don't you pick up your
    phone?—
'Cause I've got a crush on Obama—
I cannot wait, 'til 2008—
Baby you're the best candidate—
Up in the oval office
—You'll get your head of state—
I can't leave you alone—
'Cause I've got a crush on Obama

                                    —Obama Girl

When a Republican wears a little American flag lapel pin, what is he trying to say?

Dalik Chakloma
Chicago, IL

ANSWER: It depends which side of his suit jacket he's wearing it on. If it's on the left, he's saying that he's pretending to be patriotic and could actually care less about America, unless there's a no-bid contract somewhere in it for him. If the flag's on the right lapel, it means he's gay.

Clearly we live in an age where it's not what you *do* that counts, it's how you *accessorize*. When politicians wear American flag pins, it mollifies the public and sets their minds at ease knowing that these politicians don't support Al Qaeda. Just as long as they're wearing the American flag, they can give tax cuts to the rich, allow companies to pollute the air, and start unnecessary wars in distant lands.

I'd prefer that our elected representatives, instead of wearing flag pins on their lapels, wore little buttons that told us something truthful about themselves. Such as:

"ASK ME ABOUT ROBBING YOU BLIND!"

"I SUCK AT REPRESENTING YOU"

"I HAVE NO IDEA WHERE BASRA IS"

"I'M PACKING HALF A BRAIN"

"KISS ME IF YOU'RE A LOBBYIST"

All this nonsense over lapel pins began when Internet rumors started flying that Barack Obama was refusing to wear one. Instead of responding by instantly putting one on and making up some excuse that he'd accidentally dropped the other one down the bathroom sink, he gave this honest answer:

You know, the truth is that right after 9/11, I had a pin. Shortly after 9/11, particularly because as we're talking about the Iraq War, that became a substitute for I think true patriotism, which is speaking out on issues that are of im-

portance to our national security, I decided I won't wear that pin on my chest. Instead, I'm going to try to tell the American people what I believe will make this country great, and hopefully that will be a testimony to my patriotism.

He kept the pin off his lapel for an astounding 6 months after that comment. Finally, one day after a veteran handed him a pin, he quietly put it on and has been wearing it regularly ever since.

 **I heard that when the National Anthem is played, Barack Obama squats and takes a dump. I probably won't be able to vote for him if that is true.**

Penny Alger
Catonsville, MD

ANSWER: I've heard this rumor, too! And I've heard all his supporters' lame explanations for it: "His leg had fallen asleep and he was trying to wake it up," and "He was doing a dozen deep-knee bends to show his love of America." Maybe it's as simple as every time he hears "The Star Spangled Banner," he has to go. I knew a guy who every time he heard the words "Yo quiero, Taco Bell," it was a race to the can. And that was *before* he ate the Taco Bell.

These Obama rumors don't just stop with the squats. I, like many of you, have also heard the following rumors about Obama:

1. During the Pledge of Allegiance, Obama has often been seen playing with his Slinky. He used to do the whole Rubik's Cube during the Pledge, but someone told him it made him look too smart and "elitist." So he began occupying his time with games from his childhood. One time he got fellow America-haters Dennis Kucinich and Barbara Boxer to play Twister with him while the flag was being raised.

2. Once, at a Fourth of July celebration, Obama stripped down to his underwear, climbed the flagpole, and screamed at the top of his lungs, "Death to America Ferrera!" (I think this rumor explains why he

did so poorly with Hispanics in the primaries.)

3. At Ronald Reagan's funeral, Obama went up to the deceased president's body and tried to tickle him. Secret Service quickly led him away. No charges were pressed thanks to Nancy Reagan, who offered that "Ronnie would have liked it."

4. On a fact-finding mission to Afghanistan, Obama mooned an entire regiment of troops. On his butt cheeks he had painted the words "Bin Laden Hiding Inside."

5. Asked to sing "God Bless America" at Comiskey Park, Obama instead launched into a *French* version of "Total Eclipse of the Heart."

These are but a few of the many rumors about Barack Obama showing disdain for our flag, our country, and the lapel holes in our suit coats. With so many rumors, you just know that some of them *have* to be true. Why else would they be on the Internet?

If Obama can't bowl, how can he govern? I'm remaining an undecided voter until I see if he can swim and play hockey.

Mike Gates
Fond du Lac, WI

ANSWER: It *is* true that a man who can't bowl a game of 200 or above is a man who can't rule the world. Obama's gutter balls were, admittedly, embarrassing. It would have been so much better for all of us had they put bumpers in the gutters like they do for the kids.

Instead, our enemies were treated to the pathetic sight of a candidate for the American presidency unable to throw a 12-pound ball down an 83-foot lane. I am told that terrorist groups immediately posted the video of that fiasco on their websites. Jeez! Didn't Obama understand the international significance of what he was doing? Bowling is a metaphor for 21st-century world domination. The pins are the rest of the world (the African pin, the Muslim pin, the Jewish pin, the Hispanic pin, the Chinese pin, the French pin, etc.)—and the freakin' ball is the U.S. of A.!

AND WE BOWL ONLY STRIKES!!

This is how the world is. We knock 'em down, they rise up, we knock 'em down again. There's something about that logic Obama just doesn't get.

Having witnessed his pitiful performance at the Pleasant Valley Recreation Center in Altoona, Pennsylvania, I began to worry about Obama's other athletic skills. For instance, can he play hockey? That, too, is an American contact sport (don't write me about this, Canadians—you had your chance, but your greedy hockey owners sold your teams to such snow-ravaged towns as Phoenix and Tampa, so it's our sport now). I don't know if I can vote for Obama until I see him lace up and slap shot his way down the ice at Joe Louis.

After proving his hockey prowess, I will also need to see if he can swim. Why? You know why! IT'S SINK OR SWIM! I don't want "sink" leading this country. I want a master of the butterfly stroke on guard for us 24/7.

Finally, has Barack Obama ever personally rotated the tires on his car? Because that's what separates us from the terrorists. There is not a single video of any terror cell rotating the tires on their vehicles. If Obama can't get his car up on some cee-ment blocks, then, really, what good is he? PEOPLE! HEAR ME ON THIS ONE! I speak for that male, uneducated-but-hard-working vote everyone says Obama can't get!

I'm Catholic but, like Obama, I have a crazy pastor. My pastor says that women—get this—should not be allowed to terminate a pregnancy! I know—crazy! But he keeps saying it, over and over. Should I quit my church, too?

Betsy Hill
Framingham, MA

ANSWER: No. Your pastor is a man. He belongs to an institution where women are not allowed to be pastors. Women are viewed in such high esteem in the Catholic Church that your good pastor is not allowed to be in love with any of them, let alone marry one of them.

It's not just that your pastor is against abortion. He is the representative of an institution that has this to say about birth control:

The Church has always taught the intrinsic evil of contraception, that is, of every marital act intentionally rendered unfruitful. This teaching is to be held as definitive and irreformable. Contraception is gravely opposed to marital chastity; it is contrary to the good of the transmission of life (the procreative aspect of matrimony), and to the reciprocal self-giving of the spouses (the unitive aspect of matrimony); it harms true love and denies the sovereign role of God in the transmission of human life.

—Vatican Pontifical Council
for the Family, 1997

And in case you were wondering, this ban on the "evil" of contraception includes condoms, too. With the Church's political influence throughout the world, there is no telling how many people have died as a result of their condoms-are-a-sin policy.

Surely, though, when it comes to embryonic stem cell research, the Church that Jesus founded has a compassionate position, considering how such research may lead to saving millions of lives? Think again. The United States Conference of Catholic Bishops calls the harvesting of such stem cells a "gravely immoral act."

Of course, just because someone goes to a church, it doesn't mean they agree with everything the pastor preaches. A Pew Research Center survey has found that the majority of Catholics believe that abortion should be **legal** in ALL OR MOST CASES. The majority of Catholics also approve of stem cell research.

As for birth control, the Conference of Catholic Bishops estimates that 96 percent of married Catholics practice some form of birth control. Whoa. Talk about not paying attention on Sunday morning!

A recent Gallup Poll found that, in addition to not listening to the pastor's admonitions on abortion and birth control, 63 percent of all Catholics are in favor of letting their priests go out on a date, get married, and have sex (but only with a woman; unfortunately, most Catholics, according to the same poll, don't like their priests with other men).

But why don't we turn to the man himself—Jesus Christ, formerly of Nazareth—to see what he had to say about abortion and birth control, two practices that were common in his time:

Nothing.

That's right. There is not one single word in the Gospels where Jesus bothers himself with abortion. Or birth control. Or whether his apostles could have a wife. Or whether his apostles had to be only men. And on and on and on.

So don't leave your beliefs or your church behind because of what the pastor is required to preach. I'm sure if your pastor could speak from the heart, he'd agree with what I have just written. And if he wouldn't, then he's just making stuff up.

 *Hey, I have a wild pastor, too! Except mine says Jesus took seven loaves of bread and two fish—and fed 5,000 people with it. I've tried this at home and it doesn't work. Should I quit my church?*

Sue Kinter
Salem, OR

ANSWER: Yes. If you fail to understand that these Bible stories are just that—*stories*—then there's little sense in going to church, because you are going to be continually confused. Have you heard the one about the guy who set up house in a whale's stomach? Or the one where some woman looked back to say goodbye to her town—and she turned into a friggin' pillar of salt?!

The idea of these stories and parables was to help people lead a better life and get through their daily struggles. Most weren't meant to be taken literally.

If you're looking for the literal, there's plenty of reality TV you can watch. But church and the Bible are there for your self-improvement and spiritual enjoyment, not for helping you cook up a couple fish and feed 5,000 people. If you want the Cliff Notes version of all this, it's pretty simple: Jesus wants you to love your neighbor as yourself, do unto others what you would want them to do to you, love your enemy, and take care of the least fortunate. That about sums it up. Oh, and play bingo.

 *I was surprised to see a woman running for president this year. When did they start voting?*

Bud Jones
Orem, UT

ANSWER: They've been voting for about 88 years now—can you believe it?! The Founding Fathers had no use for women. They enacted legislation that said married women had no civil rights—those all belonged to their husbands. Married women had no right to own property, and any income they earned was considered the property of their husbands. Married or single, women were prohibited from going to most colleges. They were taxed but had no say in how those taxes could be spent. Women were to obey men, defer always to men, and their position was slightly above that of a slave. They weren't hung if they tried to escape.

Beginning in the early 1800s, a number of women decided they'd had enough. They began demanding equal rights, starting with the right to vote. In 1878 and 1914, amendments to the Constitution were introduced that would allow women to vote. Both failed (as do all first attempts to right a profound wrong). Women committed acts of civil disobedience and walked into voting booths. They were promptly carted off to jail. Today there are 2,372,647 women still alive who were born under this system of apartheid. Many of them had hoped this year to

29

witness the ultimate payback—a woman who would become president of the United States.

It almost happened. But Hillary Clinton made one sad and fatal mistake in the run-up to the 2008 election year. She voted to give George W. Bush the power to invade Iraq. And for the next four years she kept voting for the war. By the time she started to run for president, nearly 70 percent of the country was against the war. And Senator Clinton was on the wrong side. She tried to change, tried to sound anti-war, but never admitted her mistake, never said she was sorry. Thus, she lost the nomination to another historic candidate—Barack Obama.

Why would Hillary Clinton vote for an illegal war? My guess is her advisors told her that America would be too afraid to elect a woman unless she proved that she could kick ass and start wars just like a man. They convinced her that people (men) don't think a woman can defend the country.

It was a total misreading of the American public. I believe Hillary Clinton went against her own heart, and her reckless, calculated decision helped to send more than 4,000 of our soldiers to their deaths. She knows that wars of aggression are wrong. Her mistake cost her the election—and the chance for those 2.3 million elderly women to see a final act of justice near the end of their lives.

 *Everyone knows Ohio sucks. Why is everyone saying it will once again get to decide who the next president is?*

Drew Ashanti
Ypsilanti, MI

ANSWER: It doesn't have to come down to Ohio—or Florida—again. We need a new strategy. Here's an idea:

Forget Ohio and Florida. Assume, to begin with, that no blue state will go red this year. Then concentrate on New Mexico, Nevada, and Iowa. Win these three Democratic-leaning states, and Obama is in the White House. Win newly-blue Colorado on top of those, and he'll have an extra 8 electoral votes to spare.

New Mexico went for Gore and has a Democratic governor (Richardson) who endorsed Obama. Nevada is home to the Democratic majority leader of the U.S. Senate. Iowa ignited Obamania, and it, too, went for Gore. Kerry lost Iowa by a margin of less than 1 percent (10,060 votes).

And Colorado represents a trend in the Mountain West that shows each new generation leaving the Republican Party behind. Montana now has two U.S. senators who are Democrats (as is their governor). Arizona has a Democratic governor, as does Kansas (of all places). And Colorado has a Democratic governor, a Democratic U.S. senator, and 4 of their 7 members of Congress are Democrats.

I recommend an excellent book, *Whistling Past Dixie,* by political science professor Thomas F. Schaller. In it, Schaller writes that we need to quit worrying about winning elections in the South. We can win by concentrating on the traditional blue states and the emerging democracies of the Mountain West and Southwest. The South will eventually catch up due to so many blue state people moving there and bringing their wild and crazy blue state ideas with them. Plus, with a higher birthrate among people of color, whites will make up a dwindling percentage of the population. And that can only be a good thing.

And then, finally, there's just the simple fact that mean, old, conservative people eventually get old enough and die. All those people who started the trouble we're still in because they voted for Ronald Reagan? Well, the majority of people who were in their fifties then and voted for him are now six feet under. Gone. Can't vote from the grave.

And the succeeding younger generations have grown up to be *not* like them. They don't believe the earth was made in six days. They don't care about the race of the person they date. They hate war. And their movement this year has made it possible for an African American to be nominated for president of the United States. If you had asked any of those Reagan-loving old farts back in 1980 if they thought a black man could get elected president, they would have looked at you with a strange, confused expression, and then they would have punched you.

Things do get better. Forget the South for now. And forget poor ol' Ohio. Or not. After all, Kerry only came up 118,601 votes short in Ohio in 2004.

And a good number of those voters are dead now, too. Just like Woody Hayes.

MIKE'S ELECTION GUIDE

In the last election, Republicans were able to get out the vote by placing proposals on state ballots outlawing gay marriage. Now look at this photo—who on earth would want to outlaw THIS?

Greg Houston
Asbury Park, NJ

ANSWER: *Exactly.* Had the anti-gay marriage forces run ads with scenes like the one above, none of those gay marriage bans would have passed. I'm told that *no one* is opposed to watching two women kiss. Men love it, women love it, and the women doing it love it—something for everybody!

I don't think it's female-on-female love that has so many people (men) so discombobulated. I think when they say they are against gay marriage, what they *really* mean is that they are against this:

Now that's disgusting! Guys going all broke-back on each other—gimme a break! The state can't sanction that.

Which is too bad. Because the statistics show that gay—and lesbian—marriages last just as long as heterosexual marriages. Gay couples also do a great job raising the kids, and, don't worry, the majority of kids raised by gays grow up to be on our team. And if you've got a gay couple in the neighborhood, well, your property value just went up, 'cause you can pretty much bet that their house is going to be the nicest one on the block. How about crime? Well, how many women have to worry about a gay guy jumping them? Or a lesbian? I've never encountered a gay gang trying to jack my car or a marauding band of lesbians doing B & E's.

Come to think of it, as with abortion, Jesus never said one word about homosexuals or gay marriage. So how did all these good Christians end up in charge of the gay discrimination movement when their leader and founder left them no instructions about beating up on homosexuals?

Maybe it's time to conquer this final frontier of bigotry. Let the gays get married. And if you can't stand to look at two men making out, just pretend it's two women.

Ahhh, now isn't *that* better?

I heard John McCain once flew into a rage. Do you know what set him off? Did he ever calm down?

Mark Gotleib
St. Louis Park, MN

ANSWER: *Once?* This guy is known for going bonkers over the slightest of annoyances. But is it allowable to question a presidential candidate's mental fitness to occupy the highest office in the land, if not the world? He might get mad at you.

I think it's a legitimate question for you to ask. They raked Bill Clinton over the coals for his behavior and they published photos of John Kerry riding a windsurfer. So I will attempt to answer your question.

It appears more than a few of McCain's Republican colleagues in the U.S. Senate have commented on his temper and instability over the years. In January of 2008, Republican Senator Thad Cochran of Mississippi had this to say about McCain:

The thought of his being president sends a cold chill down my spine. He's erratic. He's hotheaded. He loses his temper and he worries me.

A chill down the spine? You have to understand that Cochran is considered to be a soft-spoken southern gentleman and is not prone to hyperbole in the Senate. When he made this comment, people knew he would not be saying it unless he meant it.

Cochran also told a reporter about the time he remembered being with McCain on a diplomatic mission to Nicaragua. They were sitting at a table with the president of Nicaragua and suddenly McCain reached across the table, grabbed a government official by his collar and lifted him out of his chair:

I don't know what he was telling him but I thought, good grief, everybody around here has got guns and we were there on a diplomatic mission. I don't know what had happened to provoke John but he obviously got mad at the guy and he just reached over there and snatched him.

None of this sounds very surprising about the senator from Arizona who likes to sing "Bomb-bomb-bomb, bomb-bomb Iran" in public.

Republican Party officials had heard enough from Sen. Cochran and, in the summer of '08, they apparently got hold of Cochran and reeled him in. His tune changed. Through Sen. Cochran's spokesperson, he said:

. . . though Sen. McCain has had problems with his temper, he has overcome them. Though

Sen. Cochran saw the incident he described to you, decades have passed since then and he wanted to make the point that over the years he has seen Sen. McCain mature into an individual who is not only spirited and tenacious but also thoughtful and levelheaded. As Sen. Cochran said yesterday, he believes Sen. McCain has developed into the best possible candidate for president.

I wonder now what they are going to do to New Hampshire's former Republican Senator Bob Smith to get him to retract this comment from April of 2008:

His [McCain's] temper would place this country at risk in international affairs, and the world perhaps in danger. In my mind, it should disqualify him.

Smith added:

I've witnessed a lot of his temper and outbursts. For me, some of this stuff is relevant. It raises questions about stability. . . . It's more than just temper. It's this need of his to show you that he's above you—a sneering, condescending attitude.

I've lost count of how many staff members Mc-Cain has fired during the 2008 campaign. First there was John Weaver and Terry Nelson, then it was Russ Schriefer and Stuart Stevens, then Bill McInturff, and then Doug Goodyear, Doug Davenport, Eric Burgeson, and Craig Shirley, and for good measure, Thomas Loeffler. He's had one "shake up" after another. The latest (as this guide went to press) was the demotion of Rick Davis.

How could someone go through so many "close" advisors and key staff people in such a short period of time if something about him wasn't a little "off"? Nothing about this seems stable, and the McCain-loving media haven't quite known how to handle it because they've spent so much time fawning over him since the 2000 campaign. For them to do an honest, hard-hitting story now would make their audience wonder where the heck they've been.

I've wondered for some time why hardly anyone has reported this statement from McCain, spoken loudly and freely while riding in 2000 with the press in his Straight Talk Express:

"I hated the gooks [referring to the Vietnamese] and will continue to hate them as long as I live."

And then there was the time at a private GOP meeting in 1999, when McCain went up to fellow Republican senator Pete Domenici and said, "Only an asshole would put together a budget like this. I wouldn't call you an asshole unless you really were an asshole."

McCain's temper, sadly, isn't unleashed on only his Senate colleagues, staff, or political opponents. According to Cliff Schecter in his book *The Real McCain,* three reporters confirmed that while on the campaign trail McCain's wife came up to him, tousled his hair, and said, "You're getting a little thin up there." According to Schecter, "McCain's face reddened, and he replied, 'At least I don't plaster on the makeup like a trollop, you c***.'"

It's almost like you don't want to go any further, you want to just stop right here and say, "Well, ok, maybe it's not a good idea to have this guy's finger on The Button. Is Mitt Romney still available?"

Why did the Vietnamese shoot down John McCain and put him in prison for five years? He seems like such a nice guy.

Rose NgBacThiu
Seattle, WA

ANSWER: I'm guessing, in spite of his anger management issues, he is a nice guy. He has devoted his life to this country. He was willing to make the ultimate sacrifice in the defense of our nation. And for that, he was tortured and then imprisoned in a North Vietnamese POW camp for nearly five-and-a-half years.

Sadly, McCain's sacrifice had nothing to do with protecting the United States. He was sent to Vietnam along with hundreds of thousands of others in an attempt to prop up what was essentially an American colony, South Vietnam, which was being run by a dictator whom we installed.

Lest we all forget, the Vietnam War represented a mass slaughter by the United States government on a scale that sought to rival our genocide of the Native Americans. The U.S. Armed Forces killed more than two million civilians in Vietnam (and perhaps another million in Laos and Cambodia). The Vietnamese had done nothing to us. They had not bombed or invaded or even sought to murder a single American. President Johnson and the Pentagon lied to Congress in order to get a vote passed to put the war in full gear. Only two senators had the guts to vote "no." Almost three million troops ended up serving in Vietnam. The United States dropped more tons of bombs on the Vietnamese people than the Allied powers dropped during all of World War II.

In response, during the nine years of the war, not a single Vietnamese bomb was dropped on U.S. soil, not a single Vietnamese terrorist attack took place in the USA. But we poured 18 million gallons of poisonous chemicals on their villages and rice fields. The number of injured, wounded, and severely deformed Vietnamese has never been counted because it's just too huge for anyone to calculate, let alone comprehend.

And yet, with all the death and destruction we visited upon the Vietnamese, we lost the war. They never gave up. Just as I'd like to think *we* would never give up should we ever be on the receiving end of such a horrific assault from an invading force.

During Christmas of 1972, though the U.S. was only a month away from calling it quits, President Nixon ordered the carpet-bombing of the civilian population of Hanoi and Haiphong. Two thousand combat sorties dropped 20,000 tons of bombs in a final burst of anger for having been beaten by a nation of peasants who didn't possess a single attack helicopter or bomber plane during the entire war.

John McCain flew 23 bombing missions over North Vietnam in a campaign called Operation Rolling Thunder. During this bombing campaign, which lasted for almost 44 months, U.S. forces flew 307,000 attack sorties, dropping 643,000 tons of bombs on North Vietnam (roughly the same tonnage dropped in the Pacific during *all* of World War II). Though the stated targets were factories, bridges, and power plants, thousands of bombs also fell on homes, schools, and hospitals. In the midst of the campaign, Defense Secretary Robert McNamara estimated that we were killing 1,000 civilians a week. That's more than one 9/11 every single month—for 44 months.

In his book, *Faith of Our Fathers,* McCain wrote that he was upset that he had been limited to bombing military installations, roads, and power plants. He said such restrictions were "illogical" and "senseless."

"I do believe," McCain wrote, "that had we taken the war to the North and made full, consistent use of air power in the North, we ultimately would have prevailed." In other words, McCain believes we could have won the Vietnam War had he been able to drop even *more* bombs.

And thus it was on October 26, 1967, that John McCain, flying in his A-4 Skyhawk, was hit by a North Vietnamese anti-aircraft artillery shell just as he fired off his missile at—not a military target, not an army unit, not a battleship—but an electricity generating station that supplied electrical power to a number of neighborhoods. The target, according to McCain, was in "a heavily populated part of Hanoi." Heavily populated. A plane from the sky raining missiles down on a heavily populated area of a nation's capital.

McCain's plane plunged into a lake not far from the presidential palace. With three broken limbs, McCain was drowning. Vietnamese civilians on the shore dove in to save him. Just like we would do, if someone had just bombed our neighborhood, right?

He was brought ashore and an angry mob formed. They beat him and someone stabbed him in the groin. That's when Mai Van On, the local villager who helped pull McCain out of the lake, stepped in to save him a second time. He stood in front of McCain and told the mob to back off. Eventually, the police and the army showed up, McCain was apprehended, and it was off to prison for him.

So let me ask the question again. If someone had just been dropping bombs on your home, how would you react? After seeing your child blown to pieces, what would you do to the man who fell out of the sky, the man who committed this act? Please answer honestly.

And if you did decide to let him live, what kind of justice should be handed to him? Should it be the death penalty, the same death penalty we are asking for those charged with 9/11 crimes in Guantánamo Bay? Or should it be life in prison? Would five years be enough? Torture is ALWAYS wrong, even when we do it. Torturing John McCain was outrageous and appalling. I hope the people who perpetrated these heinous acts have apologized to him.

John McCain is already using the Vietnam

47

War in his political ads. In doing so, it makes not just what happened *to him* in Vietnam fair game for discussion, but also what *he did* to the Vietnamese. Considering what the Republicans were willing to do to smear war hero John Kerry in the last election, I don't want to hear them now say that John McCain's war record cannot be called into question. I would like to see one brave reporter during the election season ask this simple question of John McCain: "Is it morally right to drop bombs and missiles in a 'heavily populated' area where hundreds, if not thousands, of civilians will perish?"

Please explain the electoral college. Can I get in with a 2.0 grade point average?

Rob Thomlinson
Elkhart, IN

ANSWER: The electoral college is not an institution of higher learning but rather a brilliant attempt by the Founding Fathers to build in one last layer of "protection"—just in case "the people" choose the wrong president.

Each state is assigned a certain number of electors. That number is the total sum of each state's members of Congress. Which means that the smaller states have an unequal advantage as they each have two senators, regardless of their population. This was one of many steps that the authors of the Constitution took to make sure the itsy-bitsy states got to have *more* say as to who the president should be. And really, isn't that the right thing to do, to give more power to lovely little places like Delaware?

In all but two states (Nebraska and Maine) it's a winner-take-all affair, meaning that the delegates to the electoral college are not proportional to the actual number of popular votes each candidate receives. So if Candidate "A" in Indiana got 5 million votes but Candidate "B" got 5 million and one votes, Candidate "B" gets 100 percent of that state's delegates—and Candidate "A" receives nothing.

And why should he? He *lost*, and this is America. It's written in the Constitution that we don't like losers. I think.

Denying representation to 49.9 percent of the public, though, was still not enough protection for the Founders. They built in one more genius safeguard. Let's say in Indiana they have 11 delegates assigned to the electoral college. Candidate "B" wins by one popular vote, so he gets all 11 delegates. Well, who picks the 11 delegates? The state political parties do! But that's not the best part. Any one of the 11 delegates has the legal right to vote for whomever he or she wants at the electoral college! Because maybe the people of Indiana just didn't know what they were doing and voted for the wrong candidate. Perhaps they didn't realize that the country would be much better off with Candidate "A." Eleven appointed political glad-handers are there to save the people from themselves.

And after all, who would know better about what's best for "the people" than some nameless, faceless schmuck of a political hack eating greasy pizza in the electoral college meeting room at the Holiday Inn off Exit 17 on the Indiana Turnpike?

Why do Iowa and New Hampshire go first? I don't know anyone from there.

Bill S. Nelson
Louisville, KY

ANSWER: That's because no one lives there. On the evening of December 10, 1957, unidentified flying objects were spotted hovering over both states. It is believed that the residents of Iowa and New Hampshire were abducted and replaced with seemingly harmless, but white, people. Their only supernatural power seemed to be their uncanny ability to know who, exactly, should be president of the United States. The rest of America suspected that these were not mere mortals, but said nothing because of the fine job the Iowans and New Hampshirites did selecting presidents.

True, some folks questioned the wisdom of all this. But those who dared to defy the power of these aliens, most notably the states of Michigan and Florida in 2008, were met with swift and painful repercussions. These two states attempted to hold their primaries before New Hampshire and Iowa had theirs. As a result, each Michigander and Floridian was turned into half a human for the balance of the election year.

It seems like anyone can run for office. Is that a good idea?

Sahri Gupta
Dearborn, MI

ANSWER: No. But there's nothing we can do about it. Other than quit voting for the wrong ones. The funny thing is, you can never find a politician who will admit he's the wrong one. Or a voter who will admit that he or she blew it. Try to find someone to say they voted for Bush or Nixon. Crickets. But *somebody* voted for these guys—*twice.*

So how do we stop the wrong people from running for office? I'll tell you how. Remember those weaselly weird kids who always ran for class president or student council? They should have been stopped right then and there. Because they grow up to be the awful politicians we can't stand. It was our responsibility back in junior high to smack the devil out of them and give them a good swirly—but we didn't.

Had we, they might have given up their political aspirations right then and there and, later in life, simply got a job in HR.

"Ask Mike!"

How did voting start? Who cast the first ballot?

Richie Bouton
Uniontown, PA

ANSWER: Voting began nearly 2,500 years ago in the first democracy, what we call "Greece." Actually, Greece back then was 1,500 city-states along the Mediterranean and Black seas. From what we know of them they liked sports, ate a low-carb Mediterranean diet, and bathed with each other. They wrote the first plays, invented the art of philosophy and, if they were having a bad day, they killed themselves. Antidepressants hadn't yet been invented.

The oldest and most stable of these city-states was Athens. The Athenians did not want to waste their time with "representative" democracy, which required electing other people to, um, represent them. They believed in *direct* democracy, a crazy-cool way to give everybody a say and make sure that everyone is treated equal.

Well, not exactly "equal" in old Athens. Only men over the age of 18 could vote. Slaves and women were apparently given other chores.

But for those guys in their tunics, here's how it worked:

The public directly voted on all laws and policies instead of electing politicians to make laws. The Greeks figured, "Why do we need the middlemen? We don't need professional politicians to make our decisions for us."

This concept was so radical that the word "democracy," after the Greeks were conquered by the Romans, became the dirtiest word in politics for the next couple thousand years (until the word "liberal" was invented).

But for the Greeks it worked. This is not to say the Greeks didn't have public officials. They did. But they were chosen "by lot," or at random. Anyone who wanted to be in charge of the Parthenon or director of public baths just put his name in a hat and then names were drawn. The Athenians thought this was the fairest way to do it, because it gave every candidate, whether rich or poor, famous or unknown, an equal chance of holding office.

This wasn't always the most efficient way to do things. Often they would pull a name out of the hat and it would be a Harriet Miers or a Heckuvajob Brownie.

When it did come time to pass laws, thousands would show up. Anyone could speak. As they didn't have to rush home to watch *CSI: Sparta,* they had lots of time to debate the issues. Each side had their best orators who would give their positions, and then after everyone had a chance to speak, they would vote and that would be that.

It is commonly believed that the first Greek to cast a vote was a man by the name of Chadean Anastasias Gianopolis, around the year 482 B.C. He was so eager to be the first to vote that, when he thrust his arm forward to vote "aye," he lunged so hard he fell over the railing. His long white robe caught on the rail and wrapped itself around his neck, leaving him hanging over the edge and instantly choking him to death. This is believed to be the origin of the term "a hanging chad."

MIKE'S ELECTION GUIDE

Excuse me, but was that the first pun you've ever written?

Si Green
Berkeley, CA

ANSWER: Yes. I'm not quite sure what came over me. I have never trafficked in puns and I detest all who do. Them and those who unnecessarily alliterate. It won't happen again.

Why should I vote? It only encourages them.

Red Malokowski
Red Hook, Brooklyn

ANSWER: This is true. The more you show up to vote for politicians, the more they think you like what they do. Of course, if you didn't vote, then the only ones who would show up at the polls would be the politicians voting for themselves. Which means they would always win. So not voting isn't a solution.

But where does voting get us? In most elections, 97 percent of the members of the House

of Representatives who run for re-election are returned to Washington. That is a higher return
rate than the old Soviet Politburo had, where only
91 percent of its comrades were returned after
each election. What does it say about our country when politicians behind the Iron Curtain
had a better chance of being removed from office
than they do here in the Land of the Free?

If voting doesn't really change anything, then
isn't it a little bit like recycling your plastic soda
bottles? It makes you feel like you're doing something important and necessary, but in the long
haul it isn't really dealing with the root of the
problem. The questions we should be posing are,
"Why are we using petrochemicals to make soda
bottles? And why are we drinking soda in the
first place?"

Likewise, if 97 percent of Congress that runs
every two years gets re-elected, what kind of
message is that? "Good job, boys! More war!
More poor! We don't need health insurance!
I want to pay *more* for gasoline!" That's what
we say when we line up like lemmings at the
polls and convince ourselves we're doing our
patriotic duty by voting for the same old boys'
network.

Just once, wouldn't you like to vote FOR someone instead of AGAINST him?

I suggest that from now on when you vote for a candidate you see that as only the *first* step in the process. Then commit yourself to following their voting record, sending them emails and letters, and promising to work for their ouster if they are not representing you.

Otherwise, just voting for them is a waste of time. It's like handing your teenager the keys, taking away his condoms, and saying, "Have fun! Do what you want! See you in two years! We promise not to call or bother you!"

I'm a little light in the pocket right now. Can my vote be bought?

Joe Ventura
Grass Valley, CA

ANSWER: Actually, it works the other way. Politicians do not pay *you*—*you* pay them. And whoever pays them the most, gets the most things done.

For instance, if you send a check for $25 to a presidential candidate, he or she will greatly appreciate that. But not as much as if you send them $4 million, like the energy & oil industries have given so far to the Republican presidential candidates, and the nearly $3 million they've given to the Democratic presidential candidates. Or the $8 million the big security and investment firms have given to Senator Obama, and the $5 million they've given to Senator McCain. By giving them each a large amount of money, this guarantees that Exxon Mobil or Morgan Stanley will get the laws they want enacted and maybe even help them avoid prosecution when it's discovered they cooked the books.

There have been many examples of this recently. For instance . . .

Ever wonder why lawmakers are so afraid to pass even modest gun control laws? It's not because of people like you and me, who are able to bag bucks, squirrels, and turkeys without using armor-piercing ammo or a semi-automatic assault rifle. No, it's because the National Rifle Association and its fellow gun-hugging organizations have handed out more than $17 million to federal lawmakers over the past several years, with the vast majority of that money channeled to Republicans' pockets. Do gun-control advocates really think their paltry $1.7 million in contributions over that same time period is going to buy them quality gun-control legislation? Get real! We live in a free market economy where you get what you pay for, and $17 million sure buys a lot more political clout than $1.7 million.

And . . .

Thanks to a $300-million lobbying effort by the banking industry, then-Senator Phil Gramm authored legislation that repealed important federal banking regulations in the late 1990s and also cleared the way for the big Swiss bank UBS to gobble up its competition. The deregulation policies Gramm championed led to lax government oversight of investment banking, and many economists connect this to one of the biggest financial disasters in the country: the $200 billion sub-prime mortgage mess.

(Oh, by the way, after his Senate career, Gramm went on to become a Vice Chairman at UBS in 2002. He registered as a lobbyist in 2004, and has lobbied Congress as recently as 2007 on mortgage crisis legislation. He's now one of Senator McCain's top economic advisors, the campaign co-chairman. There's speculation that, if elected, McCain would appoint him to serve as Treasury

Secretary. But that was before Gramm said that the American people were "whining" too much about the economy. As this book goes to press, Gramm was still the co-chairman of the campaign but was running things from a spider hole in Alaska.)

You get what you pay for in American politics. All 25 bucks gets you is a guarantee that every presidential speech will end with that phrase that makes you feel all warm and gooey and patriotic: "God bless the United States of America!"

Cough up a lot more and you've got a front row seat at the trough.

 *Is it true Democrats drink from a sippy cup and sleep with the light on?*

Debbi Steffen
St. Ignace, MI

ANSWER: Yes. They're a frightened bunch, and I'm not sure I know why. The American people handed them control of Congress in a stunning victory in November of 2006. Maybe that's the answer: the Democrats were so stunned by actually winning for once, they still haven't recovered.

So, yes, they still sleep with the light on. Some

want you to read them a bedtime story and then read it to them again, and again. Others just want to hug their Barney dinosaurs and play "let's be nice" with their Harry Reid action figures.

The Democrats have had nearly two years to cut off funding for the war—and haven't. They've had nearly two years to stop the oil companies from gouging us—and haven't. Their excuse is that, "Well, daddy will just veto anything I do!" Maybe daddy will, but your job is to be the voice of the American people, not do what daddy wants you to do.

The Republicans are the opposite of this. That's why most Americans like them. Guts. Grit. No apologies. Stand up for what you say you believe in, no matter how crazy or wrong it is. The public finds something cool about that and thus would prefer to vote for someone who bravely stands for their beliefs as opposed to a party that backs down and wimpers every time we need them to do the right thing.

All we can do is hope that this childish behavior will change after the election. If not, we will just have to take their thumbs out of their mouths, turn out the light, and let them cry themselves to sleep.

"Ask Mike!"

OK, so our electoral system is a mess and the Democrats are a bunch of wimps. But America can still kick ass, right?

Fred Trimble
Stone Mt., GA

ANSWER: Um, no. I mean we used to. And we'd like to think we still can.

But the truth is that we have turned into a bunch of sickly, clueless, useless wimps. If we were attacked tomorrow—I mean REALLY attacked—we wouldn't know the first thing about defending ourselves. It's a good thing we're still clinging to 10,000 nuclear warheads, 'cause if our dirty little secret ever got out, we'd be doomed!

Two-thirds of us are overweight, and if we ever are invaded, just how long do you think we'd last in our Scooter chairs? The CDC predicts that one in three of our children—one in two of our Latino children—born in 2000 will become diabetic in their lifetime simply because of their poor diets and lack of exercise. Where oh where will we find the next group of healthy recruits for the next war?

63

In fact, having 45 million of one's own people with no health insurance is not the best way to be prepared if you need to fight back. Shouldn't the first rule of any homeland security policy be a fit and healthy nation—*just in case!* In other words, my conservative friends, don't support universal healthcare because it's the morally right thing to do—insist upon it to protect your own ass!

In addition to being too fat and too sick to defend ourselves, we have also turned into a bunch of wimps. A friend of mine was telling me how his son was only allowed to throw 38 pitches at his Little League game—because Little League rules these days limit how many pitches kids can throw *so they don't hurt their arms!* Hurt their arms throwing a baseball? Do you think Al Qaeda is worried about their kids' arms? Hell no!

This overprotection of our children has reached a fever pitch. Children are watched like hawks. Every minute of their day, including playtime, is scheduled by the parents. Every little sore throat could be pneumonia. Every C grade becomes the end of the world. And if they seem a little fidgety, give them a pill. If they seem a little rebellious, give them two pills. And if they are sometimes sad, get them to a shrink—quick.

Whatever happened to "Go out in the street and play!"?

Out in the street, where there are . . . cars?

Yep. That street. Where we all played as kids. Sure every neighborhood lost someone, but it toughened everyone else up. Can you imagine Al Qaeda worrying about their kids playing in the streets?! Don't let the terrorists win!

While more of us live in fear and keep guns in our houses because of some misbegotten belief that those guns will protect us from a "home invader," fewer and fewer of us actually know how to accurately fire them. Hunting license applications are decreasing each year. Contrary to the perception that we are a nation of rednecks with gun racks on the backs of our pickups, the truth is most of us don't have a clue as to how to properly fire a weapon at a screaming terrorist coming our way. We go to bed each night with the belief that enough of the poor in need of a job have signed up to defend us. Yes, the same poor people who are among the most unhealthy and out-of-shape and who haven't seen a doctor in years, if ever.

Well, here's the bad news: The military is having a hard time hitting its recruitment goals, and standards for new recruits are sinking to new lows. Gee, I wonder why? Starting unnecessary wars that send up to 100,000 kids home from the service without eyes, arms, and legs is not the best recruitment strategy.

Ok, so we can't defend ourselves and we won't have enough poor kids to do it for us—so what are we to do?

Here are a few ideas:

1. No more play dates for the kids. Let them fend for themselves and make their own arrangements with other kids. Let them run loose around the neighborhood playing "Al Qaeda vs. Army."
2. Close down all McDonald's. Make it illegal to sell a soft drink in a container that holds more than 8 ounces. Stop all corn subsidies and bring back good old-fashioned sugar (see Chapter 3 of this book).
3. One hour of each workday becomes mandatory for exercise and firearms training. Rich bastards who wish to be defended against the impending Al Qaeda attack must pay to have their employees ready to defend them and their possessions.

4. Shut down the Scooter Store. Unless you are paralyzed or severely disabled, you are to get up and walk, using your own two legs.
5. Little League pitchers can throw as many pitches as they want until the coach pulls them outta the game. And when the game is over, the kids can walk home. In the street.

 Mike, if I have to move north of the border after the next presidential election because McCain has won, what do I need to know about Canada and Canadians?

Tami Lane
Norman, OK

ANSWER: Well, first of all, don't even *think* of leaving us behind to deal with another god-awful frickin' mess! You're staying here just like we all are! Call us masochists or call us Americans but we're here for the long haul, buddy.

Ok, listen, I feel your pain. Who hasn't at one time or another in the last eight years thought about making like Rocket Man and flying off with Major Tom? It sucks to watch the country you love being shoveled into the gutter and made either the laughingstock of—or the most hated force in—the Empire.

But if you have to head north after a (gulp!) McCain victory, here are a few tips that could be useful, based on living most of my life within earshot of a nonstop loop of Gordon Lightfoot:

1. Canadians will subtly say the opposite of what they mean, often keeping a straight face. It's called "irony." They also apply this in a form of humour (bring a lot of "u"s with you) known as "satire."
2. Canadians have very little desire to wreak violence upon you—unless you have a puck they want.
3. You will need to learn the metric system (this should be reason enough to convince you to stay here). And you'll never truly master it, thus holding up the line at Tim Horton's every single day.
4. You will not need to learn French. The Canadians will claim to be a bilingual people, and you will see a lot of signs in English and French, but don't worry—it's just

for show so that the people in Quebec don't split off and join Greenland. In fact, if you do move to Canada, move to Quebec. They're so pissed at everything, you'll feel right at home. None of them will speak English to you, so if you're looking for some peace and quiet, Quebec is your place. Eventually you'll pick up French and that will allow you to move again (when you've had your fill of Canadian politics) to that other country we all want to move to—France!

5. Finish any dental work you're in the middle of before you leave the U.S. While the Canadian healthcare system is much better than ours (it's free, it's for everyone), they don't cover dental. Enter the country with good teeth and you are guaranteed to live two years longer than if you had stayed in the USA.

6. Get ready to listen to a lot of complaining. Things are so good in Canada, after a while people there tend to take it for granted that 40 million of their people don't live in poverty—heck, they don't even *have* 40 million people! The crime rate is low, the

schools are decent, and the chocolate is real. But they get bored easily and, with no real problems to bitch about, they start making shit up. Like the Irish and the British, they absolutely hate it when one of their own ends up doing better than everyone else. They'll tear him to shreds. This keeps many afraid of doing well, and that's why no great inventions since the telephone have come out of Canada.

7. They still drink like a sieve and smoke like a stack. I don't know why this is. See #6.

8. Learn whatever you can about American government and history before you head there because whatever you think you know about America, they will know more. It's uncanny and it's scary. But I guess that's why they've studied up on their next-door neighbor.

'Cause their neighbor is sorta scary.

2

How to Elect John McCain

Or, How Many Democrats Does It Take to Lose the Most Winnable Presidential Election in American History?

A blueprint for how to blow it.

"Let's snatch defeat from the jaws of victory." "We never met an election we'd like to win." "Why get elected when you can be defeated!"

These have been the mantras of the Democratic Party. Beginning with their stunning inability to defeat the most detested politician in American history, Richard Nixon, and continuing through their stunning inability to defeat the most detested politician in the world, George II, the Democrats are the masters of blowing it. And they don't just simply "blow it"—they blow it *especially* when the electorate seems desperate to *give* it to them.

After eight years of Ronald Reagan in the Oval Office, the public had seen enough. The Democrats chose Michael Dukakis as their nominee.

71

Two months before the election, he was ahead of Bush I in the polls. Then he went to an army tank factory in Michigan, put on some kind of stupid-fitting helmet, and rode around in a tank with a goofy smile on his face. Weeks later, when asked what kind of punishment he would like to see be given to someone who might rape his wife, he started mumbling some sort of bleeding heart gibberish instead of just saying what anyone would say: "I'd like to tear the bastard from limb to limb!" The voters were so put-off by his wimpiness, they elected an actual wimp over him, George H.W. Bush.

For years now, nearly every poll shows that the American people are right in sync with the platform of the Democratic party. They are pro-environment, pro-women's rights, pro-choice, they don't like war, they want the minimum wage raised, and they want a single-payer universal healthcare system. The American public agrees with the Republican party on only one major issue: they support the death penalty.

So you would think with more than 200 million eligible voters, the Dems would be cleaning up, election after election. Obviously not. The Democrats appear to be professional losers. They are so pathetic in their ability to win elections they even lose when they win! Al Gore won the 2000 election, but for some strange reason, he didn't become the President of the United States. If you are unable as a party to get the landlord to turn over the keys to a house that is yours, what the hell good are you?

Well, in 2006, the Dems had a come-to-Jesus meeting with themselves and, under the leadership of Rahm Emanuel, won so many House seats they just waltzed in and took the place over. What a great day that was, seeing Nancy Pelosi bang the gavel down to open Congress.

And what was her first act? To declare that ANY discussion of the impeachment of George W. Bush was verboten and no one was to ever bring it up again. And that was that. It sent a clear message to Bush that he could just keep doing what he'd been doing for the first six years. The result? That's exactly what he did, with Congress authorizing every war funding bill he sent to them. How did the American people respond? Congress's approval rating sank *lower* than Bush's. How disgusting do you have to be to sink lower in the public's eyes than a man who can't even successfully choke himself on a pretzel?

So when you hear Democrats and liberals and Obama supporters say they are worried that Mc-Cain has a good chance of winning, they ain't a-kidding. Who would know better than the very people who have handed the Republicans one election after another on a silver platter? Yes, be afraid, be very afraid.

After the debacles of Iraq, Katrina, gas prices, home foreclosures, our standing in the world, the failure to capture bin Laden, and revealing the identity of a CIA agent in an act of revenge, it would seem that Barack Obama should be on a cakewalk to 1600 Pennsylvania Avenue. The man should be able to sleep his way through the rest of the campaign season.

Ha! Think again. How many Democrats does it take to lose the most easily winnable election in American history? Not many. Just a few "close advisors" to Barack Obama who tell him a bunch of asinine stuff and he ends up listening to them instead of his own heart. As the party hacks in the past two elections have proven, once they get the candidate's ear, the rest of us might just as well order pizza and stay inside the next four years.

In an effort to help the party doofuses and pundits—and the candidate himself—spare all of us another suicide-inducing election night as the results giving the election to the Republican pour in, here is the blueprint from the Democrats' past losing campaigns. Just follow each of these steps and you, the Democratic Party establishment, can help elect John Sidney McCain III to a four-year extension of the Bush Era.

What the Democrats Can Do to Get McCain Elected:

1. *Keep saying nice things about McCain.*

Like how he's been "good on global warming" and campaign finance. Keep reminding a country at war that he and he alone is a war hero. Not to mention just an all-around good guy. Say that enough, and you know what happens? The same thing that happens when you repeat over and over "Apply directly to the forehead . . . Apply directly to the forehead . . ."—people start to believe it! You've sold them on the idea that McCain isn't a bad egg, and they do NOT hear the rest of what you have to say: *"But John McCain is four more years of George W. Bush."* If you keep saying he used to be a "maverick," our less-attention-span citizens only hear the "maverick" part, not the past tense verb included in that sentence.

This is not to say that you should in any way demean John McCain as a human being or as an American. Disagreeing strongly with his policies or the direction he would lead the country is not the same as denigrating him as a person. This particular style of politics is the cesspool that the Right and the Republican Party apparatus swim in. We do not further our agenda by imitating them. Fight, fight back, and fight hard—but fight clean. It's ultimately what I believe the majority of Americans would like to see.

There is also nothing wrong with saying nice things about McCain's *constituency,* and you should. We want to hold our hand out to people who have voted for Republicans in the past. Many of them are tired, a good number are disgusted. They won't agree with a lot of what we stand for, but they've had it up to here with the Republicans and we should make sure our tent is big enough to welcome them in.

So if you want to help elect McCain, keep blessing him as if he were the white knight who accidentally hopped on the wrong horse. Forget to continually point out that he is truly up to no good. Keep pulling your punches. Don't remind people McCain wants to help the oil companies even *more* than Bush did. Don't bring up that he wants to outlaw all abortion. Back away from painting McCain as the guy who thinks it's a good idea to stay in Iraq until pigs fly. That way, if you keep praising him, you can send a mixed message to the less-informed who are simply not going to figure it out. When they walk into a voting booth, they will see two names on the ballot:

☐ **BARACK OBAMA**
☐ **WAR HERO**

Trust me, this ain't Sweden you're living in. War Hero wins every time.

2. *Have Obama pick a Vice Presidential candidate who is a conservative white guy, or a general, or a Republican.*

Yes, it will seem like smart politics at first.

Shore up Obama's lack of military experience with a hawk.

Be true to Obama's message that he'll be a

president for *everybody* by having him run with a Republican.

Make a pitch to the purple states of Virginia and Indiana to vote Democratic this time by putting one of their own on the ticket.

Or swing for the fences and make the red state of Ohio happy by handing the vice-presidential slot to its governor.

But by doing any of this, you will upset the base that not only must come out on election day, it must also be *active* and *work* dozens of hours during the campaign. They have to personally bring ten people each to the polls with them if we are to avoid the disasters of the past two elections. Many of them won't do this extra work if Obama picks the wrong Veep. It will suck the air out of the balloon in a big way.

Obama electrified the nation on the notion of change and hope and a new fresh direction in Washington. If he picks a running mate who screams "Same old same old," it will make it harder for him to attract all the new voters he needs to bring to the polls to win. Remember that there are nearly 100 million adults who choose *not* to vote. That is a large base from which to draw millions of new votes. Obama should not desert a strategy that has worked well for him.

There is nothing wrong with picking someone who can help him win a swing state or someone who has more experience than he does in certain areas. But when I hear pundits say, "He has to pick a Catholic," well, John Kerry was a total Catholic and the Catholic vote went to Mr. W. I mean, here's one of the largest groups in the country—66 million Catholics—and they/we have only allowed one Catholic to be president in 208 years. You would think they would have been flocking to Kerry in 2004. THAT IS NOT THE WAY PEOPLE THINK. IT IS THE WAY PUNDITS THINK. Keep listening to them and you can help elect John McCain the next President of the United States.

3. *Keep writing speeches for Obama like the one in front of the American Israeli lobbying group the day after the final primaries.*

Here's what he said:

> *"The danger from Iran is grave, it is real, and my goal will be to eliminate this threat."*

and

> *". . . Let there be no doubt: I will always keep the threat of military action on the table to defend our security and our ally Israel. Sometimes there are no alternatives to confrontation."*

Sounds like a speech McCain would give. Sounds like he's ready to invade Iran. He staked out an even worse position for the Palestinians vis-à-vis Jerusalem than the one held by George W. Bush. Keep that up and more and more supporters will be less and less enthused. It will be harder to keep the base motivated if they continue to hear how Obama wants to expand Bush's "faith-based" initiatives, doesn't have a health plan that covers everyone, and wants to send more troops to Afghanistan. The implied message of all of this is that the Republican plan is a good plan. So why would voters want to elect the candidate imitating the Republican when they can get the real thing? Talk like this gets McCain elected.

4. *Somehow forget that this was a historic year for women and that there is more work to do.*

Obama should be making a speech about gender like the brilliant one he gave on race back in March. Millions of people, especially women, had high hopes for the candidacy of Hillary Clinton. Attention must be paid. And you don't pay attention to it by having your advisors run your wife through the makeover machine, trying to soften her up and pipe her down. Michelle Obama has been one of the most refreshing things about this election year. But within weeks of the end of the primary season, the handlers stepped in to deal with the "Michelle Problem." *What* problem? She speaks her mind? She wears what she wants? She thought he was crazy to run for president and tried to put her foot down? Only a *crazy* person would want her husband and family to be chewed up and ground through the political grist mill.

Michelle's biggest sin, according to the punditocracy, was to say that, as a black woman, this may be the first time in her adult life she's been really proud of her country. Shock! Surprise! Outrage! But not from any of the black women *I* know. You have to be white and stupid to not know what she was really saying. If you don't understand, let me ask you this: Have you been proud of what this country has been doing in the past few years? Are you proud your neighbors had their house taken from them? Are you proud to be sending a good chunk of your paycheck to the oil companies so they can post record profits? Are you proud to know your vice president outed one of our spies and put her life and the lives of others at risk? If not, well you're no better than Michelle Obama. That's all she was saying—what we are all feeling.

Barack Obama, outnumbered in his household 3-1 by the female gender, has a lot at stake in making sure that women's rights and opportunities are on par with men's. As one who knows what it's like to be in a class of people who traditionally have not held power, he's in an excellent position to speak to another group that has been left out—women—and assure them that he will be their advocate.

Plus, this is just good politics. Women vote by a larger margin than men. And if it remains true that Obama will not carry the white male vote (as most of the polls indicate he will not), then he simply cannot win without capturing a strong majority of the female vote. Jimmy Carter and Bill Clinton both lost the white male vote but won the White House. They did so by winning an overwhelming percentage of the black, Hispanic, and female vote. That HAS to be Obama's strategy to win. Otherwise, Cindy McCain will be our new First Lady.

5. *Show up to a gunfight with a peashooter.*

Convince yourself that the Republicans are just going to roll over and play dead because there is simply no life left in their Party. Convince yourself *this one is in the bag!* Convince yourself that if you play by the rules, the Republicans will, too.

And when McCain and his people roll out their nuclear arsenal on you, just go all sweet and sensitive and logical. Believe that the truth shall prevail, that good people will see what the Republicans are up to. As they smear you, your family, your religious beliefs—cower, back down, go on the defensive.

If they say you should quit your church, quit your church! If they explode over your speaking the truth about the anger and despair of the white working class, take it all back! Heck, if they don't like your new I'm-running-for-president logo, denounce it, apologize for it, and fire the person who designed it.

But don't stop there. Be ready to jump and change *anything* at a moment's notice. If they tell you to pull your kids out of *that school*, do it. If they tell you to change your toothpaste, don't question it. And if they ask you to stand on your head and do the hokey-pokey, snap to it and do it with a smile on your face and don't forget to apologize for not doing the hokey-pokey earlier, you meant no disrespect and please don't take it as any indication that you do not love your country, your flag, and your Christian God.

Do all of that, and then listen for that sound—the sound of your supporters shuffling away in silence. Don't worry, though—they won't vote for McCain. They'll just stop showing up at the campaign headquarters over on Maple Street. They'll say they're too busy to go on another three-hour door-to-door literature drop. They'll still take a list of a hundred voters home to call and read the index card over the phone about "why you should vote for Obama"—but there won't be much enthusiasm in their voice, and the voter on the other end of the line will hear that. After 15 or 20 calls, they'll give up—after all, there's dishes to do and a dog to walk. And on election day, they'll go do their duty and vote, but they will not be up at 6am driving around the city's neighborhoods picking up strangers who need a ride to the polls.

And some of them, well, they've seen it all before, one Democratic loser after another. One more dashed hope, one more realization that the war won't really end and life will continue to just get harder. On the way to the polls, they might just come to a stop light and, after 10 seconds or so of all of this welling up in their head, they might just say, who needs this, turn around and go home. Maybe they'll pick up a six pack on the way. Maybe there's a new episode of *Deal or No Deal* on tonight. That would be nice. The girls are pretty, especially the blonde in the third row. Wait, they're all blonde. No, not that one—THAT one! Oh yes, I see her. She *is* pretty. But the Man in the Booth has picked up the phone! He's calling down to you. Deal? Or no deal? No deal! No deal! Don't do it! Hey, I'm outta beer! Why didn't I pick up a case? Now I gotta spend 8 bucks on gas to go buy more beer! Aaaaarrrgggggghhhhhh!!!! HOWIE MANDEL ISN'T WEARING A FLAG PIN!! U-S-A! U-S-A!

6. *Denounce me!*

The candidate Obama, at some point, might be asked this question: "Michael Moore is a supporter of yours and has endorsed you. But in his new book, *Mike's Election Guide,* he says the following (go ahead and fill in the blank—I've provided a full list of outrageously offensive lines *already taken out of context* in advance to make it easy for right-wing commentators, Fox News, and Dr. Sanjay Gupta). Will you still accept his endorsement or do you denounce him?"

And he better denounce me or they will tear him to shreds. He had better back away not only from me but from anyone and everyone who veers a bit too far to the left of where his advisors have told him is the sweet spot for all those red state voters. I won't care and I won't take it personally. After all, I'm not the guy who married him or baptized his kids. I'm just the idiot who went to the same terrorist Muslim school of flag pin desecrators he went to.

I remember poor John Kerry not even being able to admit, when asked by Larry King, if he had seen *Fahrenheit 9/11.* "No," he said, "I haven't. . . . I don't plan to, right now." *But he had indeed seen it.* I sat there watching him say this and I just felt sorry for him and for the election he was about to lose.

Months later, as I toured the country in my own independent effort to get him elected, we both arrived in Albuquerque the same day, each of us holding a separate rally. One of us had 7,500 people show up in the University of New Mexico basketball arena; the other had 800 come to an airport hangar. All I remember is feeling really bad about it. It did not feel good that we knew he was going to lose.

So Barack, by denouncing me, you can help McCain get elected. Because when you denounce me, it's not really me you're distancing yourself from—it's the millions upon millions of people who I agree with and who feel the same way about things as I do. And many of them are the kind of crazy voters who have no problem voting for a Nader just to prove a point. Elections have been lost by just 537 votes. I don't want that to happen to you.

We can't take four more years of this madness. We need you to be a candidate who will fight back every time they attack you. Actually, don't even wait 'til you have to fight back. Fight first!

Show some vision and courage and smoke *them* out. Take the offensive. Keep asking why these lobbyists are McCain's best friends. Let's finally have a Democrat who's got the balls to fire first.

Or tell the press you've had the boys from Chicago "remove Michael Moore to an undisclosed location, and that will be the last you hear from Mr. Moore until after the election."

3

Ten Presidential Decrees for His First Ten Days

Mr. Obama, here are ten good ideas you
can announce once you are inaugurated,
one for each of your first ten days in office.

1. *Bring Back the Draft.*

We all know that the U.S. occupation and war in
Iraq would have been over a long time ago if there
were a draft. The streets would have been full of
protestors every single week. Imagine the reaction
on college campuses if students were suddenly being drafted and dumped into the boot camps of
the United States Army. Whoa! If you think those
Obama rallies have been huge, just try sending all
those young people to Tikrit.

Of course it would never would have got to that
point because their parents are opposed to this war
(that's 63 percent of the country) and would never

have allowed their children to be shipped off to die for W.

But . . . if it's *someone else's* kids doing the dying (as it is in this war), well then, the streets are quiet, the electorate subdued.

The new president needs to bring back the draft. But with a twist:

Draft only the 18-to-26-year-old children of the richest people in America—those whose earnings put them in the top 5 percent of income earners.

That's right. Draft the rich.

There is no better way to know if a war is truly necessary than to see if the wealthy are willing to sacrifice THEIR OWN OFFSPRING. And the day they are, we *all* better sign up 'cause that can only mean some scary shit is coming our way!

Do you think we would invade a country that posed no threat to us if the rich kids had to die? How many more of these needless wars do you think we'd have if there was an assembly line of bodies from our upscale suburban and private schools right into the military?

What's the one thing we know about the rich and their kids? They like to live! They like to live because life is *good!* The only time they would even give the slightest thought to risking their precious platinum-plated lives is if someone was at the door threatening to kill them and take all their stuff. If there were no servants around to fend off the attackers, no safe room to hide in, then I think I can actually see them using whatever means they had available to stop the intruders.

Like they did in World War II. Rich people such as Joe Kennedy, Jr., famous athletes like Ted Williams, and numerous movie stars, including Jimmy Stewart and Henry Fonda, joined up to serve. Even the President sent his sons off to war to defend the country. They perceived Hitler and Tojo to be a real threat to their existence. So everyone—including and *especially* the rich—joined in the war effort to defeat the fascists and the aggressors.

Therefore I can assure you that, back in 2003, had the rich thought there was even the *slightest* chance they would never see Aspen again, they would have had their sons right there on the front lines with the kids from Detroit and South Central and Appalachia. Bush would have sent his daughters off to do their duty, as would've the pro-war senators Hillary Clinton and John Kerry, each of whom had daughters of draft age at the time.

But, strangely, none of them went. Of course

they didn't! They knew the war was a ruse, that no real threat existed and that there was no need to sacrifice their children. Only one senator voted to send his enlisted son off to war, and he was a Democrat (Tim Johnson of South Dakota).

But would we be able to front a full military with just the offspring of the well-heeled? I did the math to find out exactly how many rich kids, 18 to 26, we have in this country. Our current military has 1,372,905 enlistees. And guess what? *There are 1,305,675 wealthy offspring of draft age in the U.S.!* So we would have virtually the same size armed forces using *just rich kids!*

Think about it. Who would be more incentivized to go out there and defend America than the youth who will benefit the most from it! And you can bet daddy's little rich girl isn't going to be driving around Fallujah in some tin can Humvee. That vehicle is going to be made of solid titanium forged from Grandpappy's Brazilian mines. There will be no line out the door at the V.A. hospital when the sons of CEOs come home with no legs. They'll have private rooms with catered meals and beautiful nurses.

We need to start drafting the people who will make sure we never have to go to war.

2. *Anyone Who Tries to Make a Profit From Healthcare Will Be Arrested.*

Being able to see a doctor when you're sick should be a human right. It's a life and death issue, the same as if your house was on fire or you were a victim of a crime. And just like our free and universal fire and police protection that is afforded to every citizen, health insurance should be provided FREE OF CHARGE TO EVERYONE.

And it is—by every other civilized government on earth except ours.

This is a matter of national security. An unhealthy nation full of overweight, diabetic weaklings who are so sugared up they have no idea where the front door is so they can go out and run around and get some fresh air, *has no way of defending itself!*

There must be, in the United States, a universal healthcare system that is run by one government agency (like Social Security) and is nonprofit. It must cover everyone who lives here, no exceptions. It must contain a heavy focus on prevention. Dental and mental must be treated the same as medical.

Private profit-making insurance companies

and profit-making hospital chains should not be allowed to exist in this system. No American should be denied medical services because a company doesn't see a profit in it, and likewise no corporation should be able to gain from others' illnesses.

Systems like the one I'm describing here cost nearly 50 percent *less* per capita than the one we now have—and yet they provide *better* care than we do. In each of these Western industrialized countries that have universal healthcare, their people live longer than we do here in the USA. If the promise was one of a longer life for less money, who wouldn't jump at the chance of that?

Barack Obama and John McCain, that's who. Neither believes in true universal healthcare that covers everyone—and most importantly, one that cuts private, profit-making, greedy health insurance companies out of the picture. The thing is, I know why *McCain* wants to protect corporate profiteering. For some reason, Obama does, too. "Why?" would be a good question to ask him if you see him.

There is a bill in Congress that does for America the very thing that is done for every other citizen in the Western world. It's called HR 676, the

United States National Health Insurance Act, sponsored by Rep. John Conyers. Ninety members of Congress have signed up as co-sponsors. It is the law that needs to be passed. Americans will still be able to pick their own doctor and go to whatever hospital they want. No one can be turned away.

The corporate army of public relations spinmeisters will fight this legislation with everything they've got. They will tell you that it's "socialized medicine." You tell them that you like your "socialized fire department." They will tell you that you will have a longer wait to get help. You tell them, "Oh, you mean longer than the six hours I spent in the waiting room of the ER last week with my kid, or the six-month waitlist I'm on to see a dermatologist?" They will say that pharmaceutical companies won't have the money to research and discover new life-saving drugs if they can't charge $300 for a prescription. You say, "You mean the life-saving drug that was developed with my tax dollars at the University in Ann Arbor (only 17 percent of the research for our drugs is done by the drug companies)?"

We would not allow the police to ask us for a credit card before they start looking for the crook who broke into our home, and we would not allow the fire department to demand a fire insurance card before they start putting out the fire. We should make it illegal for anyone to say to a sick person, "Will that be cash or charge?"

3. Ban High Fructose Corn Syrup.

One way to help us live a bit longer would be to ban the most evil substance known to man: high fructose corn syrup.

Read the label of anything you're eating and you'll probably see the words "high fructose corn syrup" somewhere. It's in everything and you can't get away from it. Just because the word "corn" is in it, please don't think for a second that you're getting one of your five recommended vegetable servings of the day. High fructose corn syrup has as much to do with corn as I have to do with the Boston Marathon.

High fructose corn syrup is a super sweet and very cheap "sugar" extracted from corn without any of that silly corn fiber, taste, or nutrients. Real sugar is not cheap. Back before the 1970s, that's what food manufacturers used in their products. And they tried to use as little as possible because the more they used, the more it cut into their profit margin.

Then along came Richard Nixon.

In the early 1970s, Nixon, who was already under immense political pressure because of the Vietnam war, was beginning to see waning support from a traditionally strong Republican base: farmers and big agribusiness. They were upset because a series of short-term economic problems were putting a serious squeeze on their income.

In the midst of this crisis Nixon brought in former Purdue University dean of agriculture Earl "Rusty" Butz to serve as America's eighteenth Secretary of Agriculture. Butz, who had a penchant for telling tasteless jokes and bemoaning welfare spending, turned his attention to eliminating anything that got in the way of farmers planting "from fencerow to fencerow." But what would they do with all this corn? Sell it and make it into high fructose corn syrup (HFCS). Because real sugar was expensive. HFCS, derived from cheap and widely available corn, was a bargain.

As a result of Nixon's and Butz's corn policies, the average American has gone from consuming zero pounds of HFCS per year in the late 1960s, to 63 pounds per year in this decade.

Thanks to $19 billion a year in subsidies to agribusiness giants making food products that harm Americans, we are a sicker—and poorer—nation as a result. Because of all these subsidies, every dollar of profit ADM makes on corn sweetener costs consumers and taxpayers $10.

Thanks to all this cheap and easy high fructose corn syrup, soft drink and fast food companies have turned 8- or 12-ounce drinks into 16- or 20-ounce super-sized drinks or 32-ounce Big Gulps. While turning cheap corn into HFCS has resulted in cheap soda, cheap corn can also be used in making burgers and other fast-food or processed junk foods. Cheap, subsidized corn, in the form of HFCS, is the backbone of our ever-growing national waistline.

If you look at the charts, you can see when the obesity boom began in the U.S. It began with the introduction of high fructose corn syrup into our diet. If you are overweight you are in the majority—two-thirds of us are now overweight, and a third of us are actually obese.

This weight gain has increased the risk of heart disease, turned millions into diabetics, and generally reduced the quality of most people's lives.

It has probably also killed more people than Nixon did in Vietnam. It is our domestic napalm.

So who better to issue the ban on high fructose corn syrup than the skinniest man ever to win the presidency! You *know* his mother never fed him any of this crap. Remember the Friday night during the primaries when John McCain finally released his medical records—over 1,100 pages explaining everything that's gone wrong inside his body.

The following week, Obama released his medical records. Total number of pages? One. *ONE!* One friggin' page. All it was was a letter from his doctor saying he'd quit smoking and there was absolutely nothing wrong with him, never has been anything wrong with him, and—my favorite—a sentence stating that he has "no excess body fat."

What better leader to get us all healthy and fit again? That should be reason alone to elect this guy. And when he issues his decree banning the corn syrup, he should do it with his shirt off. And then tell everyone at home watching to "drop and give me ten."

It will definitely be a new day in America.

4. *The American People Will No Longer Pay More Taxes Than the French Do.*

What if the new president proclaimed on Inauguration Day, "Beginning this year, you will pay *less* taxes than the French."

At first, people would go, "Hey, we already pay less than the French!" One thing we all know is that not only the French, but most Europeans, pay more taxes than we do. They have to because they must pay for their socialized welfare state, and we—well, we just get up in the morning, pull ourselves up by our bootstraps, every man for himself—enjoy one of the lowest tax rates in the world!

Sadly, this is one of the biggest lies we are told. The truth is, a typical American family pays much more than a typical French family. The reason we have gotten away by claiming the opposite is that we just change the words so that we don't call certain things a "tax."

A French couple with two children pays an average income tax of 22 percent; in the USA the average American couple with two kids pays 19 percent—less than the French.

But here's the rub. What French taxes cover and what ours cover are two very different things.

Here's what a French family's income tax gets them:

- **FREE healthcare**
- **FREE (or virtually free) child care**
- **FREE tuition at every university, from community colleges to the Sorbonne**
- **Four months minimum of maternity leave with FULL PAY**
- **Mandatory 30 days vacation each year at FULL PAY**
- **Unlimited sick days at FULL PAY for all citizens**

All of that—for paying just a bit more to the government. How can they afford that?

Here's how. They don't invade countries. They stopped being a colonial power. They don't let the corporations entirely run their country. They have strong unions. And the citizens will shut down the country if the government misbehaves.

Because we don't provide the above benefits the French get—and instead make our citizens pay for them out of their pockets—we don't refer to these fees as "taxes." *But that's exactly what they are.* Taxes. We Americans each pay our *regular* taxes, and then on top of that we pay *much, much more.*

If you are paying for your own family's health insurance, you pay an average of $12,000 a year in "premiums" (taxes), plus hundreds of dollars more in co-pays and deductibles (taxes). (If your employer pays it, that's money you could otherwise be negotiating to be paid in WAGES; plus, even with employer-funded health insurance, you still end up getting socked with the numerous co-pays and deductibles.)

When, as an American, you pay for your own college education, you're paying a tax that we call "tuition, room, and board." And if you're still paying off your student loans, you're paying hundreds of dollars each month in student loan payments (again, a tax that we don't call a tax)—often well into your thirties or forties.

And how much are you paying each year in child-care costs? That's day care, baby sitters, preschool, and other caregivers. Some pay $200 a month, some pay $400 a week. We don't call that a tax, but that's what it is. And I'm not even talking about what you are paying at your kid's PUB-LIC school for band, art, sports, driver's ed—all the stuff that used to be free. You still pay the property and income taxes for the public schools—and these days, thanks to so many corporate tax breaks where billion-dollar companies are paying either half or none of what they should be paying, you now pay a larger personal share—but you don't get the same free services you used to get.

And that, I believe, is what's at the core of our American tax dissatisfaction. We hate, and I mean HATE, paying taxes in the U.S. It's not that the French *love* paying taxes, but there is nowhere near the level of grumbling in France as there is here. And no wonder. *They actually get something in return for all the taxes they pay! Never have to worry about getting sick. Never have to worry about who will look after the kids. Never have to worry about sending their sons and daughters off to college (or off to war).*

They pay for all this peace of mind with their income taxes—and they get it back in spades.

We, on the other hand, pay all these taxes and can't even get a pothole fixed. We can't even be certain when we drop a letter in the mail it will ever reach its destination. I'm looking out the window at an empty lot across the street that hasn't been mowed all summer. Wanna catch a city bus in Detroit? Don't forget to bring *War and Peace* to read while you're waiting at the bus stop.

Instead of services to benefit us and our families, our taxes go to waging two wars, lining the pockets of military contractors, handing out welfare to oil companies that turn around and rob us at the pump, and other rip-offs.

No wonder we're mad. Meanwhile, the French are having sex.

5. *Ban All Commericals in Movie Theaters.*

Mr. President, does this one really need any explanation? When you go to the movie theater, you're there to see a movie, not a screeching ad for Chevrolet. You have left the house because you don't want to watch TV. You have paid for a baby sitter, the gas in the car, the $10 movie ticket, and the $7 popcorn. You have done so in order to escape into the magic of the cinema. But before you can watch the latest Coen Bros. masterpiece, you must first be reminded that you'd be having a lot more fun if you were sitting at home playing the latest version of Grand Theft Auto.

Because the theater chains think the public is stupid (and why shouldn't they when they see people line up at their door eager to pay ten bucks for *Saw IV*), they think we won't mind sitting there through 20 minutes of TV commercials. Remember when it was just one ad? Nobody objected, so they just kept adding more. Now whole companies are devoted to creating 20-minute packages of 30-second ads to blast at you once the lights dim and you think you're about to see a couple of previews and then the feature.

In 2007, movie theaters raked in $417 million in ad revenue from these pre-movie screenings, up 15 percent from the previous year, making this one of the fastest-growing types of advertising.

But why stop at just showing ads before *movies*? How about Pepsi commercials each day as Congress is called to order? Viagra ads on the curtain before a Broadway play? Victoria's Secret spots shown to the faithful before Mass?

The new president needs to ban all ads other than the "Coming Attractions" in our nation's cinemas. If you want to help him with a head start, let your local theater know that you did not come here to watch TV. And let the advertisers know, too. Go to www.captiveaudience.org to join the protest movement.

After enacting this ban, the new president should ensure that no bag of popcorn costs more than three bucks, that people talking on cell-phones and texting on BlackBerries will be water-boarded in the theater lobby, and that the kid popping the corn won't be the one running the $100,000 projector.

6. Defeat Al Qaeda and the Next Generation of America-Haters by Building Wells.

Let's begin by admitting there is no way to stop some crazy lunatics from blowing things up. They have always done that, and they always will do that. No amount of taking my shampoo from me at the airport X-ray machine is going to stop them.

By the way, Homeland Security, if you happen to be reading this because the publisher slipped you an advance copy in return for some unmentionable "favor," here's a little tip: The next terrorist attack is *not* going to be on an airplane. These terrorists may be nuts, but they do not have Tourette's. One thing I know about them, they're really big into "Been There, Done That." They don't like to repeat themselves. Check out their pattern:

KENYA AND TANZANIA: CAR BOMB.

USS COLE: BOAT BOMB.

9/11: AIRPLANES AS BOMBS.

BALI: NIGHTCLUB BOMB.

MADRID: TRAIN BOMB.

LONDON: BUS AND SUBWAY BOMBS.

Now that they've dispensed with all the major forms of transportation-as-weapons (assuming they have no Segway or wheelchair attacks planned), what's next?

Why wait to find out? Why not start by asking ourselves a question: "Why us?"

Why are they targeting *us?* What did we do to them besides help prop up their Arab dictatorships with weapons sales and military bases on their soil? Hey, we need the oil! You can't get all the neighborhood kids to the soccer game in a Chevette.

Is it because, as George Bush says, they're jealous of "our way of life"? Well, why don't they go after Sweden or France? They have a way-better quality of life than we do.

I guess it's pointless trying to figure out why someone wants to kill you. What isn't pointless is trying to prevent them from recruiting the next generation of America-haters. Here's a plan for the next president to dry up the growing group of enlistees of third-world poor who seem eager to harm us.

Dig wells.

Tonight, there are over one billion people on this planet who do not have access to clean, safe drinking water. Two billion people do not have a sanitary sewer system of any kind where they live. One third of the planet! These two tragedies are the number one cause of illness, disease, and death for the people of the third world.

And what is so terribly wrong about this is that we have the money and the know-how already in place to see that each and every one of them can have access to clean water and sanitation. This is not rocket science. This is not some plague for which we have no cure. It is simple, cheap, and doable. The ability to do it has been around for decades. Instead, we have let the poor of the earth suffer unnecessarily. Why? How do we answer for this?

It has been very easy for the bin Ladens of this world to point the finger at us and say, "Look what they take from us—and look at how we get nothing in return!" America has only 5 percent of the world's population and yet we grab and use 25 percent of its resources. Did we think no one would notice?

To top it off, we cut deals with many of these countries' leaders who are already oppressing their own people. And the oppressed in these countries know that.

Enter George W. Bush and his oilmen/henchmen. Mix that in with everything else and it's like we've handed those who would hurt us the best recruitment ad around.

Our new president, whose family, in part, comes from the Third World, could turn this all around with one simple decree:

"From this point forward, the United States of America is committed to being a good neighbor on this planet. We will prove that by starting with this pledge: We will guarantee that every citizen on earth has access to clean drinking water and sanitation by the year 2020. Your babies will no longer die of dysentery. Your elderly will get to live beyond their current life expectancy of 46. Your life will be better. And this will all come to you courtesy of your friends in the USA."

Not possible, you say? Too expensive? How much do you think it costs to dig a well in a Third World village? $10 per person. That's right. Ten bucks. Folks, we can do this. As for the labor, it's a much better use of our young people's time than sending them to invade countries for things that don't belong to us.

And throughout the poorest parts of this planet, where hatred of America is growing, every one of these wells and sewer systems will have the following words inscribed on them:

"Built for the people of this village as a

gift from the people of the United States of America.”

If we want, we can add an asterisk: “Please don’t hurt us anymore.”

7. *From Now On, When You Dial 4-1-1, You Will Be Talking to Someone Who Lives in Your Town.*

Hey, now *that’s* a novel idea.

When I was a child, before there was 4-1-1, you just dialed “0” for the operator. A nice lady would answer and she would say, “Operator.” And then you could ask her anything, from “What time is it?” to “Get me the police, there’s an axe murderer in my bedroom!” She was always there for you. If you asked for Billy Tomaszeski’s number down the block, she would ask how Billy’s mother was doing. If you couldn’t remember which street the Woolworth’s was on, she’d know ’cause she just bought some stockings there this morning. If you asked for the number of a place on “Gratiot and Livernois,” she wouldn’t ask you to spell either of those streets because she lived there and knew exactly where it was.

Many of you have never lived under an information system such as this. The greedy phone companies merged, broke-up, then merged again into something I have no idea what or where it is, who runs it, who works there, or if they are even still on this planet. The idea that there is anyone in your town who works for the phone company is laughable.

Replaced by robots, computers, and way-too-happy workers in Calcutta, the 4-1-1 information system is where the real joke is. By the time you've spelled and re-spelled the name for them, by the time you've explained that you're in Portland, Oregon, not Portland, Maine, and after getting a "supervisor" on the line who finally finds the number for you, you could have driven over to the guy's house you were calling and gotten the number from him in person.

Just like with anything labeled "customer service" these days, the whole point of this exercise of calling a number for help—only to get NO HELP and have your brain turn into a rototiller of rage—is to wear you down to the point that you will toss the broken electronic device you are calling about into the trash and go out and buy another one. If they were actually there to help you, then your device might get fixed and you'd be all content and happy and they wouldn't make any money.

And that, sir, is not the point of Capitalism. Capitalism is designed to have you in a constant state of unhappiness, fear, and anxiety—and living life in a brain-dead stupor. How else can you be convinced to *buy! buy! buy!?* And after what you've bought doesn't bring you happiness, how dare you call customer service and expect us to make you happy! Get back to work, peasant! Work means freedom! To shop! God forbid you should ever lose your job. No money = certain death. And death is really unhappy.

Our new president needs to issue this decree: "From this day forward, when you dial 4-1-1, you will be talking to someone who lives within 20 miles of where you live. They will help you. They know how to spell *Pascagoula.*"

(As for improving customer service at Best Buy, I'm sorry, eliminating capitalism is not one of these ten decrees.)

8. *Make Social Security Solvent Until the 22nd Century by Having the Rich Pay Their Fair Share.*

For many years now, the Republican elite has been on a singular mission. That mission has been to dismantle as much of the federal government as possible. The thinking is that by eliminating government programs that help the poor or disadvantaged, they, the rich, will pay less taxes.

That made sense to a majority of Americans, and so we have had a Republican in the White House for 20 of the last 28 years. Why would so many Americans approve of this strategy of being so cruel to their fellow, less-fortunate citizens? It's a unique thing about us—we really, REALLY hate the riffraff, the destitute, the losers. They're like lepers to us. We don't want them around us, certainly not in our neighborhoods where they will bring down our property values. We don't want to have to look at them on the street corner. We don't want their kids going to school with our little precious ones.

But mostly we turn away because, in them, we see the possibility of *our* future. We know that deep down, there but for the grace of God, that could be us. We know how cruel our system of capitalism is, winners and losers—more losers than winners—and we know that we somehow lucked out and got to scrape by on the nicer side of town.

Once the idea of taking away from the poor caught on—so much so that the Democratic administration of Bill Clinton joined in on the dismantling—the Republicans tried, bit by bit, to close down the federal government. They convinced Congress and the president to privatize everything, from taking the census to running the mess hall on an army base.

And the cutbacks resulted in a huge tax savings for the rich—$410 billion since 2001. But by privatizing services—handing these jobs over to companies who had a fiduciary responsibility to make a bigger and bigger profit each and every year—it has ended up costing more money, and in many cases, not getting the job done half as well. When you hand an ice truck over to someone who doesn't know where New Orleans is, and the ice truck is found still driving around Maine two weeks later, somebody is paying for this bill. That would be you.

And when they start a war in order to grab some oil, and that war ends up costing $2 billion a week for five-plus long years, well, the boys at the country club ain't gonna be paying for that, either. Instead, the government just borrows the money from the rich man and then expects YOU to pay interest to him for the next 20 years.

Yet so much of the middle class wants to keep voting for Republicans because they promise to keep the poor in check—when all the time the ones getting the real body check are the middle class. The poor—don't worry about them. They'll survive, they always have. And sooner or later, as history shows, they'll get fed up and come looking for us.

A nice gate around the neighborhood, anyone?

So here we are with the biggest spending administration in the history of America. They have run up a record debt, and by the time you read this it may be in Chinese 'cause that's who owns our ass now. The Commies won! Long live Chairman Mao! The same people who told us to hate the Commies are the ones who went into business with them to screw us. What dopes we are. Embarrassing.

But enough good citizens have caught on. The Republican party—a true axis of evil that figured out 30 years ago the way to rule America was to bring together the religious right with Wall Street—has now realized that their days are numbered. So in desperation, the Republicans and John McCain are once again pushing the lie that the other party is the "tax and spend" party. And they are back to proposing—ever so gingerly— that we must move toward privatizing Social Security. They reach into their bag of fear tricks and pull out chestnuts like this:

"Social Security will be broke by 2017! Government has failed you! Let us invest it in the stock market!"

Well, they're right. Social Security will be busted sooner or later. BUT NOT BECAUSE THE MONEY ISN'T AVAILABLE.

It will be broke because the rich and the near-rich DO NOT PAY ONE DIME OF SOCIAL SECURITY TAX ON ANY INCOME OVER $102,000!

Yes, you read that line right. I'll wait a moment while you read it again.

Social Security will be broke because the rich and the near-rich DO NOT PAY ONE DIME OF SOCIAL SECURITY TAX ON ANY INCOME OVER $102,000!

Got it? Anyone who makes more than $102,000 a year pays NO SOCIAL SECURITY TAX on anything they make above that. Zip. Zero. Nada.

But that's not the deal *you* get. YOU pay Social Security tax on 100 percent of *your* income! It is entirely taxed at the full 6.2 percent for Social Security.

But the upper middle class and the rich are NOT taxed at 100 percent of their income. That flat tax they love to wax on about? That's for YOU, not them. And if you're making $40,000 a year, and you have to give up 6.2 percent of your income to Social Security—no deductions or excuses allowed—that is a big bite of your income.

But if a person who makes a million dollars a year doesn't have to pay the 6.2 percent tax on 90 PERCENT of his income, well, the pain he feels is no worse than a mosquito bite.

And here's the rub—and the Big Lie of Omission—that they don't want you to ever hear:

If all Americans—including the rich—had to pay the same 6.2 percent on all their income into Social Security, THERE WOULD BE ENOUGH MONEY IN SOCIAL SECURITY UNTIL ALMOST THE BEGINNING OF THE 22ND CENTURY!

Instead of ever telling you this, they have filled you with fear that your Social Security will not be there when you retire. They have you convinced that when you are old you are going to be shit-outta-luck. They want you scared *now*, while you are young, so you will work your nose to the grindstone, work two jobs if necessary, and behave yourself so you don't lose that job. And don't ever forget about all those Democrats who are going to *spend all your money!*

Well, there is a quick and simple fix to make sure the elderly and retired don't suffer—and that's by making every American pay that 6.2 percent tax. No exclusions.

And when that happens all Americans can rest assured that there will be funds for them in their old age.

An act of Congress and a stroke of the pen can make Social Security solvent *today—and for the rest of the century.*

9. Update the Pledge of Allegiance.

As a child in Catholic school, each day began with a prayer and the Pledge of Allegiance. I understood why we were praying. There were tests to take and good grades to get, and a prayer to the Old Man might cause Him to look upon me with a smidgen of mercy.

But when it came to the Pledge of Allegiance, I was confused. Why was I pledging my loyalty to a *flag?* I knew that the flag was supposed to be a symbol, but a symbol of what? Freedom, democracy, good roads? Ok, I was for that. A nation founded on genocide and built on the backs of slaves where women couldn't vote for the first 140 years? Hmmm. I wasn't so sure about that. Also, wasn't *idolizing* a flag in direct contradiction to the commandments of the Guy we were just praying to (something like, "Thou Shalt Not Honor Any Idols, Symbols or Golden Calves Other Than Me")?

Then one day in school, while pondering the relic bones of the patron saint of floor enamel, I came up with a solution to this conundrum. But first, a little history.

Far from it being some sort of loyalty oath invented by witch hunters looking to round up the rebellious heathens, the Pledge of Allegiance was in fact written by an American socialist, Francis Bellamy, in 1892. Bellamy was also a Baptist minister. He preached radical sermons like "Jesus, the Socialist." He was a deep believer and supporter of his cousin, Edward Bellamy, who wrote *Looking*

Backward, a socialist utopian novel describing the 21st century as a workers' paradise in which people earn equal pay, work reduced hours, and retire early with benefits. It was one of the most popular American novels of its time, selling more than a million copies.

Francis Bellamy believed that good citizenship in a true democracy was the best way to emulate what Jesus preached. Bellamy had the Pledge published in *The Youth's Companion,* a popular children's magazine at the time. He asked President Benjamin Harrison to issue a proclamation in favor of the Pledge, and on Columbus Day, 1892, 12 million school children across America recited the Pledge in school.

This was the original wording of the Pledge:

"I pledge allegiance to my flag and to the republic for which it stands, one nation, indivisible, with liberty and justice for all."

Not bad, simple, to the point. But like all good ideas, some people just can't leave well enough alone. In 1924, "my flag" was replaced with "the flag of the United States of America." Then schools began requiring all students to recite the Pledge every day—and those who didn't were often punished (the perfect way to encourage love of one's country).

But in 1943, the Supreme Court ruled that forcing everyone to recite the Pledge was unconstitutional and that students could opt out of saying it.

In 1954, though, at the height of the Commie scare, the Knights of Columbus and other religious groups got Congress to add the words "under God" so as to distinguish America from all those godless communist countries. The new improved Pledge, which remains to this day, thus went: "I pledge allegiance to the flag of the United States of America, and to the republic for which it stands, one nation under God, indivisible, with liberty and justice for all."

It is now more than 50 years later, with a lot of who we are and what we've done that's flowed under the bridge. Over 80 percent of our nation now thinks the country is "on the wrong track." More than half of the world's citizens do not hold us in high esteem. Something needs to change.

Let's start with a new Pledge of Allegiance for the 21st century. It would go like this:

> *"I PLEDGE ALLEGIANCE TO THE PEOPLE OF THE UNITED STATES OF AMERICA, AND TO THE REPUBLIC FOR WHICH WE STAND, ONE NATION, PART OF ONE WORLD, WITH LIBERTY AND JUSTICE FOR ALL."*

Not bad, eh? Kinder, gentler, and in recognition that we are in the same boat with everyone else on this planet.

And let's leave it up to God if He wants to bless us. It really is His call—one I'm sure He'll make based on our behavior—isn't it?

10. Free HBO for Everyone!

If the new president would like to do just one thing to make everyone's life a bit happier, he could pick up the tab for every household to get free HBO.

Let's face it, TV is dead. It has become truly unwatchable. Other than a couple of comedies on

NBC (*The Office, 30 Rock*), a couple of dramas on ABC, and the 11pm hour on Comedy Central, the rest of the week seems like it was written by guys who eat their lunch in the crapper. The sitcoms are so stale they will soon become like vaudeville. ("What's vaudeville?" Exactly.) Extinct.

This is not to say that there are not informative shows on all those cable channels up in the triple digits. I've learned where to find the best feather pillows on HGTV, how to handle our dog when she is filled with anxiety on *The Dog Whisperer*, and how to hem a dress quickly should I ever end up on *Project Runway*.

But by and large, it would do us all a world of good to turn the damn thing off and go for a walk. Or have a conversation with a friend. Or do some laundry. Or learn to play the viola.

Of course, most of the younger generation has already turned it off and moved across the room to a smaller screen that is both a wealth of egalitarian information AND a brand new crap machine of time-killing, mind-numbing nothingness.

In the landscape of all this noise, there still remains an oasis of keen and hip smarts, a place where they never have to worry about offending a sponsor or a government oversight panel. That place, as you know, is called HBO.

On top of showing movies uncut and uncensored with no commercial breaks, HBO has produced some of the finest television in recent memory. *The Sopranos* was like the greatest of novels—a work of modern literature—and if there could be a Nobel Prize for such an effort, this show deserved it. The other HBO dramas were/are of near-equal brilliance: *Six Feet Under, The Wire, Big Love,* even *Rome* was cool and sexy and weird. The comedies, too, are great: Larry David's *Curb Your Enthusiasm, Entourage, Extras, Sex and the City*—the list goes on and on.

HBO should be free and made available to every American. (Or at least to me for giving them this unsolicited plug.)

HBO is proof that we can still do some things right as Americans. Its existence says that we are not afraid to take risks, that we are in fact NOT a nation of idiots. Thirty million of our 110 million households already have it. Let's bring the rest of our fellow citizens in on the fun and the smarts.

FREE HBO! GOD BLESS AMERICA!!

4

Six Modest Proposals to Fix Our Broken Elections

As we all know, there was no better proof of how messed up our electoral system is than when the man who got the most popular votes in 2000 (and the most *electoral* votes, had all the votes in Florida been counted) did not become the president of the United States. It was a smackdown of epic proportions to our Democracy, and one from which it hasn't recovered.

Since then, the move to electronic voting machines has only made it worse. Experts estimate that 10 percent of those machines fail at least once in each election.

Voting turnout in the U.S. remains among the lowest of all Western democracies (even though there has been a nice bump this year, thanks to the close race on the Democratic side).

And at the root of it all lies the money. No matter how many reforms have been tried, no matter how you try to color it, money rules the day. Even though the vast majority of Barack Obama's funds have come from small donors, when he first started running in 2007, the only way he could launch his long-shot candidacy was to depend on the money of rich people. Fifty-four percent of his funds in 2007 came from people who gave $1,000 or more.

The worst of all of this is that the campaign season, which used to be confined to six grueling months, has now expanded to two bone-crushing, mind-altering, soul-sucking years of our lives. Two dozen debates, hundreds of pundits run amok, the same exact speech given in every single city. Have mercy on us!

This has to stop. And it can. In some very simple, easy ways, we can spend less time, less money, and have *more* say in our future.

Thus, here are my Six Modest Proposals to Fix Our Broken Elections:

1. *Hold All Elections on the Weekend.*

Upset that you have to work 100 hours a week at your two jobs and just can't find the time to vote? Ever wonder why our leaders still think a work day is a good day for people to vote? Maybe so that not too many of those "workers" show up? The people in charge aren't stupid—if they made it too easy for the working class to vote, God knows what would happen. What if we had our elections on a Saturday or a Sunday? Well, nearly everyone might vote.

Those who have an easier time taking off to go and vote whenever they damn well please are the same people who have a vested interest in making sure those with unnecessary grievances—the poor, the uninsured, those whose kids go to substandard schools—don't flood the polling places on election day.

The United States of America ranks #139 in voter turnout of countries that have held elections since 1945. We Americans like to be #1 at everything—but #139?!

I was wondering, just how do these other countries get a bigger turnout? One of the reasons is that many of them hold their elections on a Saturday or Sunday. Check it out:

COUNTRIES	DAY OF WEEK FOR VOTE
Australia	Saturday
Austria	Sunday
Belgium	Sunday
Brazil	Sunday
Finland	Sunday
France	Sunday
Germany	Sunday
Greece	Sunday
Iceland	Saturday
Italy	Sunday and Monday
Japan	Sunday
Mexico	Sunday
New Zealand	Saturday
Portugal	Sunday or national holiday
Russia	Sunday
Spain	Sunday
Sweden	Sunday
Switzerland	Sunday

So my first proposal is that our national election day is changed from the first Tuesday in November to the first Sunday of November. That should guarantee a bigger turnout and thus our Congress and the President will be more representative of the whole country. The only reason why we vote on Tuesdays in November is because when this tradition began in 1845, it was the most convenient time for farmers to vote. It was timed for after the fall harvest and on a Tuesday because Monday was needed as a travel day to get to the polls. In other words, they set up our original elections to occur when it was least likely the majority of people would be working!

Well, times have changed, Tuesday's a work day, so let's move our election day to the weekend. It's already been proposed in Congress; Senator Herb Kohl of Wisconsin has introduced the Weekend Voting Act to Congress in 1997, 2001, 2005, and again this year. All we need is some presidential leadership to get this moving. President Obama?

2. Every Citizen Is Automatically a Registered Voter.

I was once talking to a Canadian friend before an election there, and I wanted to know whether the party he favored had a chance of winning. I asked

how their voter registration drives were going and
if they were gonna turn out a big vote. He looked
at me as if I were asking him to show me his
handgun.

"Uh, voter registration drive?" he asked.

"Yeah. You gotta register new voters and young
people if you want to have a chance of winning,"
I explained. "Aren't you canvassing, going door-to-
door, registering students, holding house parties,
going to nursing homes . . . ?"

"You do all that just to REGISTER voters?" he
asked me. "That's a waste of time and money, eh?"

"I guess. But you have to do it if you want to
win elections."

My Canadian friend explained to me that they
too, at one point, had a time-consuming, money-
wasting system that ended up leaving far too many
voters off the election rolls.

Rather than blowing all that time and money
only to end up falling short and leaving some
voters unregistered, they created a federal database that eliminated the need to go though all
that mess.

It was then that my Canadian friend hit me
with some more humbling news. "Most Western
democracies have systems like this. As a matter of

fact, most democracies have universal voter registration. The requirement for being registered to vote is just being born. Your birth certificate is, in essence, your automatic Voter I.D. card. But you don't take your birth certificate with you when you vote. You just show up and they look you up in the federal database of people who were born in Canada. So let's say you've moved recently. Or you've been out of the country for a few years. Or you haven't voted in a long time. Doesn't matter. You just show up at the polls. They have your name.

"That way, I guess you could say our voter registration is 100 percent!"

I inquired how this was possible. "You mean you don't have to stand in line at the city clerk or driver's license place to register to vote? By the simple fact that you were born in your country, this automatically makes you a registered voter 18 years later?"

"Yup."

Of course, my American mind goes right to the "what if" worst-case scenario.

"What about voter fraud? People going to different towns and voting more than once?"

"Is that your problem?" the Canadian asked me.

"People voting *too much?* Isn't your problem that you can't get Americans to vote in the first place? It seems like it's hard enough to get your country-men to even vote *once*, let alone finding Americans who would devote that kind of energy and gas money to traveling all over hell's half acre just to vote again and again!"

The Canadian was right. Why do we make people jump through hoops just so they can vote? You don't have to go sign up somewhere for the privilege of paying taxes, do you? If you work, you pay taxes. You don't have to go stand in line and fill out a form for the right to drink alcohol at age 21, do you? On your 21st birthday, you can legally drink. You don't have to prove you have been living at a certain address. If you want to have a baby, you don't have to register with any government official. You don't have to show any papers or be responsi-ble in any way. You just have to take off some of your clothes and make sure your partner is of the other gender (unless you want to be artificially in-seminated, then you can skip getting all sweaty having to listen to him mispronounce your name).

Shouldn't the simple fact you are a citizen be enough to be handed a ballot on election day? Sure a few will try to cheat, but I guarantee you that will be less a threat than continuing to have only half our citizens participating in their democracy.

3. *Use Paper Ballots. And a #2 Pencil.*

Gee, what a simple idea. Here's how it works in nearly every other high-tech, industrialized country:

A voter shows up at the polls, she or he is handed a paper ballot, the voter then goes behind a curtain where—lo and behold!—there sits a #2 pencil! The voter takes said pencil and places a mark next to the names of the candidates she or he wishes to vote for. The voter then opens the curtain, walks over to a big box, and places his or her ballot inside it. Done. No tiny holes to try and punch, no computer screen that is harder to read than an ATM machine in Tunisia, no ballot that must then be fed into an optical reader.

An optical reader! Man, are we a bunch of lazy asses or what? We'd rather trust a machine to do our reading for us? Or some computer server a hundred miles away? What happened to our own two eyeballs?

Because "those two eyeballs" is how they do it

most other places. When the polls close, the box of ballots is opened and, in the presence of a representative from each party with a candidate running for office, the ballots are placed on a big table and, in full view of everyone, the counting begins. When they are done, they often count them again. Any observer can object at any time.

How has this worked for the Canadians, the Brits, the Irish, and everyone else? Just fine. The mistake rate is practically nonexistent. Compare that to our mistake rates for electronic voting machines (2.2 percent), optical scanners (1.6 percent), or punch cards (2.6 percent). So if a hundred million Americans vote, that means that over 2.5 million of them don't get their votes counted. There is no better way to vote and count ballots than the old school way—a piece of paper, and a pencil.

But wouldn't this take too long? No. In Canada, a nation of over 30 million people—and with the second largest land mass in the world—their ballots are all counted within hours. I mean, these Canadians have to get to the polls by canoe, dogsled, or baby seal, from way up in the Yukon to the provinces that are half way to Iceland. Larger countries like the UK and France also use paper ballots (though there is a drive on in many of these countries to turn to computerized voting, this would be a huge mistake. They always want to copy us. Crazy).

Voting by paper ballot and pencil is a classic "if it ain't broke, don't fix it." We broke something. Now we need to fix it.

4. *Hold Regional Primaries.*

There is a much easier and sensible way to conduct our primaries. Instead of one state or one region having undue influence over this process (yes, I mean you aliens of Iowa and New Hampshire), we should hold just four primaries, one for each region of the country, and take turns rotating which region goes first. East (from Maine to DC and over to Pennsylvania), South (all the usual suspects, including Texas), Midwest (from Ohio to Kansas and the Dakotas) and the West (from the Rockies to the Pacific).

This way, the candidates can save time and money by concentrating themselves in just one area of the country at a time. Many of these regions share similar issues (the Midwest has water it's trying to keep clean, the West would like that water, the East desperately needs better mass transit, and the South, they'd like more NASCAR tracks). This way, everyone gets heard.

And just so we don't have to listen to a bunch of whining from Iowa and New Hampshire, we'll let them open their polls an hour ahead of everyone else so they can say they were "first."

5. *Limit the Election Season to Four Months for the Primaries, and Two Months for General Election.*

In Great Britain, the total length of the campaign for prime minister and parliament is three to four weeks. In Canada it's four to five weeks. In Slovakia it's 15 days.

Here in the U.S., it lasts almost as long as the Ming Dynasty. Months upon months have now turned into years upon years. By the time of the election, the public has grown hair in suspicious places and the pundits are down to discussing the candidates' socks.

The 2008 election officially began in 2006, and by the time we elect a new president on November 4, more than 2 million people will have died in the United States since the campaign season began. That's a lot of citizens who went to their graves getting all worked up about who they were going to vote for and yet never had the chance to have a say. Is that fair?

We need to set limits on the length of our campaign season. I propose we take the four regional primaries I've suggested and, with one month per region for the candidates to campaign in, we should know who the nominees are after just four months. No campaigning can begin until this primary season has started.

Then, after the two (and someday, hopefully more) parties' candidates are chosen, it's 8 weeks to barnstorm the country. Hold a debate every two weeks during those 8 weeks. That should tell us all that we need to know.

If we need more time than that to decide, then we've got bigger problems than this one.

6. *Public Financing, Free Air Time, and Spending Limits for All Politicians.*

By the end of 2007, a full ten months before the election, the entire pool of U.S. presidential candidates had raised MORE THAN A HALF A BILLION DOLLARS. Barack Obama alone has now raised a record $287 million as of late June 2008; McCain had raised $119 million and borrowed another $39 million. And they still had 4 months until Election Day. These guys are spending hundreds of millions of dollars to get elected to a job in which they make $400,000 a year.

Compare this to Slovakia, where presidential candidates are limited to spending 4 million Slovak crowns (about $210,000). Or Britain, where parties can't spend more than a total of £19.38 million ($38.5 million) but usually spend far less. Or France, where spending is capped at €13.7 million ($21.6 million) for candidates in the first ballot and €18.3 million ($28.9 million) for those in the second ballot. Same goes for Ireland. And Canada. And . . . well, you get the idea. They don't turn their elections into financial free-for-alls like we do.

And in many of these countries, the public foots the bill for a big chunk of the limited amount of money they do spend. For instance, in Canada if a candidate gets at least 10 percent of the entire vote, he or she is reimbursed for 60 percent of expenses. In France, if a candidate receives more than

5 percent of the vote in the first ballot, they are reimbursed for 50 percent of their spending.

With all these caps and limitations, how do candidates get the word out? What with advertising so darn expensive, how can they actually pay for all their ads? After all, during a one-month period in the spring of 2008, Obama spent $11 million on campaign commercials alone. Total ad spending during the primaries was $200 million. And the Campaign Media Analysis Group estimates that total ad spending could push past $800 million (up from $650 million in 2004) by the time this election circus finally dismantles its tents and loads the elephants and donkeys on the train headed for Election Year 2012.

According to the International Institute for Democracy and Electoral Assistance, in 72 countries around the world, including 14 Western European countries (Andorra, Belgium, Denmark, France, Germany, Italy, Malta, Netherlands, Norway, Portugal, San Marino, Spain, Sweden, and the United Kingdom), political parties are entitled to FREE MEDIA ACCESS. Same goes for Canada. It's actually *against the law* for candidates in some of these countries to purchase air time. In France, TV stations are *required* to help the candidates produce their free and equal commercial spots. In Ireland, political parties are entitled to free three-minute broadcasts aired every evening after the nightly news.

Just three minutes? Wow, sounds like the rest of the day's 1,440 minutes can then be spent in peace and quiet, candidate-free.

Any takers?

5

One Last Job to Do When the Election Is Over

On January 20, 2009, there should be
a perp walk coming out from the
West Wing of the White House.

So much negligence, so many crimes, so hard to list all the war profiteers, so little regard for the law or the Constitution—what do we do with George W. Bush and his gang of charlatans and criminals come high noon on January 20, 2009?

For more than five years, I have maintained that impeachment would be too kind a punishment for Bush and Cheney. Instead, I have advocated for a perp walk out of the West Wing of the White House, a line of men—and one woman—handcuffed and chained and being led out the door by the FBI, just like they do when they arrest a drug dealer or child abuser or Wall Street embezzler. The perpetrators attempt to shield their faces from the TV cameras by holding their windbreakers over their heads or, if they have no windbreaker, then they try to hang their head down so low you can't see the look of shame and fear in their eyes.

The purpose of the typical perp walk is to make an example of the accused, to send a simple but powerful message to the people watching at home: if you break the law, we are coming after you, we are going to get you, and you are going to be led away just like this from your good life and into a cell with bars so that we can separate you from the rest of us decent folk.

Misters Bush, Cheney, Rumsfeld, Rove, Wolfowitz, Abrams, et al.—and Ms. Rice—must not be allowed to get away scot-free. Too much money is missing, too many families have been destroyed, too much blood is on their hands. Their misdeeds are not the stuff of impeachment. That's reserved for presidents who lie about their sex lives and who try to switch secretaries of war during Reconstruction.

No, this group of leaders did much worse. They took the public's trust (which was given to them not by the public, but rather by the Supreme Court) and ran with it. They covered up the facts in order to start a war of aggression, not one of defense. They invaded a sovereign nation and removed its leader without the request or consent of that nation's people. They handed no-bid contracts to the companies they used to run and from which they still profited. They arrested people—including American citizens—and imprisoned them without a trial, without a chance to talk to a lawyer, without even knowing what the charges were against them. Some of these prisoners were tortured, not by some rogue soldiers but at the suggestion of the Secretary of Defense with the consent of the President of the United States.

Billions of American dollars were "misplaced" in Iraq, and never found. American citizens who committed no crimes were spied upon. Telephone companies were cajoled into turning over private records of innocent people.

All of this was done in response to a shocking attack on the seat of American capitalism and the seat of American military might. These were attacks that perhaps could have been prevented had anyone, especially the president himself, bothered to read the intelligence reports that said, *right up at the top of the page*: **Bin Laden Determined to Attack Inside the U.S.** Further down it referred to the possibility of hijackings.

If I am asleep at the wheel of my car and that causes the death of innocents, then I am liable, and I can guarantee you that I AM GOING TO JAIL. Forget for a moment the premeditated crimes of this administration. Just the outright negligence and incompetence of this band of C students has caused so much suffering from New Orleans to every classroom of every school in this once-great nation where nearly every child was left behind. Now a half-generation has been done in and sent down the road to social, civic, and cultural stupidity.

And if I were to, right now, right here in this book, list the name or names of covert CIA agents—an action that could lead to their death or disappearance—I can guarantee you that there will be search warrants issued, and calls will be made to try me for treason.

I say all of this with no desire for vengeance or one ounce of vindictiveness in my heart toward George W. Bush. Contrary to what many of you may assume, I harbor no hatred of him. I have never uttered the words, "I hate George Bush." Hatred of another person is a vile place to exist, and it does more damage to you than to the object of your hatred. You can hate what he does—

and I do—but to hate him as a human being is useless and often sinks you to his level.

So, my desire for his arrest this coming January 20 at 12:01pm is only about this one thing: are we a nation of laws, or not? If we are, then we will have committed a crime ourselves if we allow Bush & Co. to escape without being brought to justice. The point is not so much to imprison them because they will remain a threat to the public at large or to imprison them in order to rehabilitate them. Let's all agree on this one point: there is NO WAY to rehabilitate Dick Cheney or Don Rumsfeld. They will go to their deathbeds unrepentant and unchanged. Their fate is best left in the hands of a Higher Power.

The reason they must stand trial is to prevent high crimes such as theirs from ever occurring again. If we let them go without having to answer for their actions, trust me, we will relive this horror show with some other administration somewhere else down the line. THAT is why we must pursue indictments against them and their list of crimes. Imagine the message the perp walk will send to future presidents if they even consider starting an illegal war or raiding the people's treasury to line the pockets of their friends. I'm not talking so much about punishment of the current president as I am about prevention of the next rogue commander in chief. Is that not worth it? Is it not our duty to insist that such trials take place? Are we a nation of laws—or not?

If the answer is "not," do we leave it to someone else to set us straight? To clean up the neighborhood and rid the government of an out-of-control criminal element? How would this be done? Do we even want to consider the ramifications?

As you can see, we have no choice. We ARE a nation of laws, laws that are based on a common code of decency, of right and wrong, and, dare I say, of the religious teachings that tell us it is a sin to steal, a sin to lie, and most of all, a sin to kill. If we cannot bring ourselves to take a simple stand for everything we know to be right and good and true . . . then who are we? What have we become? And what legacy do we leave those who come after us? History will not judge us kindly, my friends, if we fail to act.

(On June 9, 2008, against the orders of his party leadership and the Democratic Speaker of the House, Congressman Dennis Kucinich of Cleveland,

Ohio, submitted Articles of Impeachment on the floor of the United States House of Representatives against President George W. Bush. Though impeachment is not ultimately what is needed, these 35 counts against the president do serve as a guide for the list of crimes and acts of negligence committed while in office by the 43rd President of the United States. For a full reading of the charges and the evidence to back them up, go to http://kucinich.house .gov/NEWS/DocumentSingle.aspx?DocumentID= 93581.)

ARTICLES OF IMPEACHMENT FOR PRESIDENT GEORGE W. BUSH

ARTICLE I

Creating a Secret Propaganda Campaign to Manufacture a False Case for War Against Iraq.

ARTICLE II

Falsely, Systematically, and with Criminal Intent Conflating the Attacks of September 11, 2001, With Misrepresentation of Iraq as a Security Threat as Part of Fraudulent Justification for a War of Aggression.

ARTICLE III

Misleading the American People and Members of Congress to Believe Iraq Possessed Weapons of Mass Destruction, to Manufacture a False Case for War.

ARTICLE IV

Misleading the American People and Members of Congress to Believe Iraq Posed an Imminent Threat to the United States.

ARTICLE V

Illegally Misspending Funds to Secretly Begin a War of Aggression.

ARTICLE VI

Invading Iraq in Violation of the Requirements of H. J. Res114.

ARTICLE VII

Invading Iraq Absent a Declaration of War.

ARTICLE VIII

Invading Iraq, A Sovereign Nation, in Violation of the UN Charter.

ARTICLE IX

Failing to Provide Troops With Body Armor and Vehicle Armor.

ARTICLE X

Falsifying Accounts of US Troop Deaths and Injuries for Political Purposes.

ARTICLE XI

Establishment of Permanent U.S. Military Bases in Iraq.

ARTICLE XII

Initiating a War Against Iraq for Control of That Nation's Natural Resources.

ARTICLE XIII

Creating a Secret Task Force to Develop Energy and Military Policies With Respect to Iraq and Other Countries.

ARTICLE XIV

Misprision of a Felony, Misuse and Exposure of Classified Information And Obstruction of Justice in the Matter of Valerie Plame Wilson,

Clandestine Agent of the Central Intelligence Agency.

ARTICLE XV

Providing Immunity from Prosecution for Criminal Contractors in Iraq.

ARTICLE XVI

Reckless Misspending and Waste of U.S. Tax Dollars in Connection With Iraq and US Contractors.

ARTICLE XVII

Illegal Detention: Detaining Indefinitely And Without Charge Persons Both U.S. Citizens and Foreign Captives.

ARTICLE XVIII

Torture: Secretly Authorizing, and Encouraging the Use of Torture Against Captives in Afghanistan, Iraq, and Other Places, as a Matter of Official Policy.

ARTICLE XIX

Rendition: Kidnapping People and Taking Them Against Their Will to "Black Sites" Located in

Other Nations, Including Nations Known to Practice Torture.

ARTICLE XX

Imprisoning Children.

ARTICLE XXI

Misleading Congress and the American People About Threats from Iran, and Supporting Terrorist Organizations Within Iran, With the Goal of Overthrowing the Iranian Government.

ARTICLE XXII

Creating Secret Laws.

ARTICLE XXIII

Violation of the Posse Comitatus Act.

ARTICLE XXIV

Spying on American Citizens, Without a Court-Ordered Warrant, in Violation of the Law and the Fourth Amendment.

ARTICLE XXV

Directing Telecommunications Companies to Create an Illegal and Unconstitutional Database of the Private Telephone Numbers and Emails of American Citizens.

ARTICLE XXVI

Announcing the Intent to Violate Laws with Signing Statements.

ARTICLE XXVII

Failing to Comply with Congressional Subpoenas and Instructing Former Employees Not to Comply.

ARTICLE XXVIII

Tampering with Free and Fair Elections, Corruption of the Administration of Justice.

ARTICLE XXIX

Conspiracy to Violate the Voting Rights Act of 1965.

ARTICLE XXX

Misleading Congress and the American People in an Attempt to Destroy Medicare.

ARTICLE XXXI

Katrina: Failure to Plan for the Predicted Disaster of Hurricane Katrina, Failure to Respond to a Civil Emergency.

ARTICLE XXXII

Misleading Congress and the American People, Systematically Undermining Efforts to Address Global Climate Change.

ARTICLE XXXIII

Repeatedly Ignored and Failed to Respond to High Level Intelligence Warnings of Planned Terrorist Attacks in the US, Prior to 9/11.

ARTICLE XXXIV

Obstruction of the Investigation into the Attacks of September 11, 2001.

ARTICLE XXXV

Endangering the Health of 9/11 First Responders.

6

Mike's Handy
Candidate Guide

**Whoever wins the White House, it will really
be about who controls Congress. Here are 12
Senate and 30 House Seats the Dems Can Win.**

While all the attention in the past year has been
on the upcoming presidential election, little notice has been given to the House and Senate races
for Congress. Every seat in the House and a third
of the Senate seats are up for grabs in November.
Republicans this year are stuck with having to defend a whopping 23 of the 35 seats that are up for
election. The Democrats, if they don't screw it up
(a caveat that I know is already implied when using the word "Democrats"), have a chance to take
real control of the Senate (which now votes 51–49
in their favor, meaning that "independent" Joe
Lieberman votes with them most of the time to
give them a nominal majority).

Whereas many of us hope that we don't end up with four more years of a Republican in the White House, we also know the chances of that happening are clearly there. We also know that, should the Democrat win, he will be fought tooth and nail by the Republicans on every piece of legislation—and will need all the help he can get.

The one way to guarantee that President Obama will have the Congress he needs in order to get his work done—and for the rest of us to have a filibuster-proof, and perhaps even a veto-proof, Congress should the Republican win—is to elect a Senate in November with at least 67 Democrats and a House with 290 Dems. This way we have an insurance policy no matter what happens in the presidential election.

So what are our chances of getting the Fool-proof Congress? Quite good, actually—if we all band together and do the work that needs to be done. Many analysts believe that the Democrats have a chance to pick up so many seats this year, it's almost ridiculous. That's because the Republicans have sunk the nation, the people know it, and a few days after Halloween the Republicans up for re-election are going to watch themselves starring in a horror movie called, *Revenge of the Voters*.

Here's the lay of the land:

Four Senate Republicans are defending seats in states where the majority of voters have consistently been voting Democratic in the past two Congressional elections and in the last presidential election. Republicans John Sununu of New Hampshire, Norm Coleman of Minnesota, Gordon Smith of Oregon, and Susan Collins of Maine are all up for re-election in blue states. The Dems need to snatch away these four seats, *plus* win the open seats in Colorado, New Mexico, and Virginia where the Republican senators are retiring. Assuming that no Democrat will be thrown out of the Senate this November (a safe assumption), the Democrats have to pick off just TWO Republican senators who are currently in red states. The most likely chances are in Alaska, Mississippi, North Carolina, and Oklahoma. It won't be easy, but if there ever were a year in which the public is in a mood to "throw the bums out," this is the year. Especially with a popular Democratic presidential candidate who's bringing millions of new voters to the polls.

This takeover will only happen if each of you reading this decides to devote a small or large chunk of your time (and a few dollars if you can) to these campaigns. You may already live in one of these states; give the campaign a call and volunteer to help. If you live in a safe area, think about spending a week or two or more in a congressional district that could use the help.

You can find out how to get involved by going directly to any of the candidates' websites or simply go online at ActBlue.com, which is the online clearinghouse for Democratic action. Their website enables you to volunteer or contribute to any Democratic candidate anywhere across America.

So let's begin by taking a look at where our best chances are to remove a few Republicans from the United States Senate . . .

Twelve Senate Seats We Can Win

COLORADO

Mark Udall

Senator Wayne Allard, Republican of Colorado, is retiring this year. In his 12 years in the Senate, he was most noted for . . . well not much. In 2006 *Time* listed him as one of the country's five worst senators, pointing out that although he serves on two powerful committees, he has actually pushed through very little legislation. With Democrats being elected by the crate-full these past four years in Colorado, Allard is wisely keeping his promise to serve only two terms.

Which is good news because the very popular Democratic congressman from Colorado, *Mark Udall*, is running for Allard's Senate seat.

Udall has worked tirelessly for a wide range of important causes, including the environment, public education, and strengthening Social Security and Medicare. He has been an advocate for protecting Colorado's wilderness areas and wrote legislation that turned the site of a former nuclear weapons plant into a wildlife refuge. Udall bravely

161

voted against giving the president authority to go to war in Iraq and was a staunch opponent of the Patriot Act. Udall is pro-choice, pro-conservation, and pro all the good stuff which will make us a better country.

Udall's Republican opponent in this election is Bob Schaffer. Schaffer must have done something right during his six-year tenure in the U.S. House of Representatives. When he quit to run for a failed Senate attempt in 2004, he immediately landed a cushy job with Aspect Energy, an oil and gas exploration company. And who better to have running against you this year than a mouth-piece from the oil and gas industry. Schaffer's only chance of winning will be if he literally gives away tank-loads of free gas to voters in the month before the election.

Back in the 1990s, Schaffer took it upon himself to personally remove AIDS pamphlets from a safe-sex display at the Capitol. According to the *Durango Herald,* "He was offended that children visiting the Capitol might see descriptions of unsafe sexual practices and a poster displaying condoms as 'Smart Sportswear for the Active Man'." Somebody should remind Senator Schaffer that although the Catholic Church has banned condom use, the state of Colorado has not.

NEW MEXICO

Tom Udall

Following the lead of Wayne Allard (and the trend in the southwest to go with the Dems), Republican Senator Pete V. Domenici of New Mexico is retiring. Domenici has been around forever—and up to no good. He supported the Bush tax cuts. Then he voted to make it harder for people to file for bankruptcy. And one of his latest acts of mischief was allegedly pressuring U.S. Attorney David Iglesias to step up the investigation of a corruption probe of New Mexico Democrats prior to the November 2006 election. Iglesias was fired six weeks after the phone call; he was one of 9 U.S. attorneys fired that year for what is widely assumed to have been political reasons.

And who better to replace Domenici than Mark Udall's cousin—New Mexico congressman, Democrat *Tom Udall*. This Udall also voted against the Iraq war. A strong environmentalist, he authored legislation to establish a nation-wide renewable energy standard in which utility companies would be required to generate a certain portion of their electricity from clean and renewable sources such as wind, solar, and geothermal. As Attorney General, he instituted an environmental enforcement division and led preservation efforts in the state. Rep. Udall also sponsored the Healthy Workforce Act of 2007, aimed at providing tax credits to employers who implement employee wellness programs.

Would you believe me if I told you that his opponent, just like his cousin's in Colorado, is an oil man?! Yep, Republican Congressman Steven Pearce came from oil and then sold his oilfield services company in 2003 for $12 million, proving that he's not only an oil man, he's stupid. Imagine if he had sold it *now?* He voted against the Alternative Energy Tax Incentives Bill in March 2008 and opposed expanding government-funded healthcare to 6 million uninsured children. He opposed increasing the national minimum wage to $7.25 (or $15,000 a year). People don't need $15,000 a year to live on! Oh, and he voted for the war. Let's send Steven Pearce back to the oil business. What better time to continue his abuse of the American people!

VIRGINIA

Mark Warner

The Republican Senator and former Mr. Elizabeth Taylor has decided to retire this year. Though voting the wrong way most of his Senate career, he will be remembered for standing up to George W. Bush during the last couple years over the war in Iraq.

Running on the Democratic ticket to replace him is former Virginia governor *Mark Warner*. Under Mark Warner's stewardship as governor, Virginia was hailed as "the best managed state in the nation" by *Governing Magazine* and the top state for educational opportunities for children by *Education Week Magazine.* Virginians gave Warner a 75 percent job approval rating when he left office as governor of Virginia in 2006. What politician gets that at the end of his term? The amazing thing is that when Warner took the helm, the Commonwealth had a $6 billion budget gap. Now, what kind of governor would leave Warner and the state with such a mess? Well, none other than Warner's opponent in this year's Senate election, former Virginia Governor Jim Gilmore.

In a showdown between former Virginia governors, Jim Gilmore belongs in the flyweight division. Having burned through Virginia's budget (and leaving it to Warner to set the state right again), Gilmore now wants a key to the vaults of the U.S. Treasury. What else does Happy Jim Gilmore have up his sleeve? A constitutional amendment banning same-sex marriage, immediate drilling for oil in ANWR, and putting conservatives on the bench.

Hopefully, Gilmore's agenda will disappear as fast as Virginia's taxpayers' money did when he was governor.

NEW HAMPSHIRE

Jeanne Shaheen

New Hampshire's Republican incumbent senator, John E. Sununu, is younger than Barack Obama, but he votes in a way that would make his old man, John Sununu, George Bush I's chief of staff, proud. He has voted against incentives for clean energy, against extending tuition deductions for college, and against expanding the child tax credit to more children. This last bill would not have cost the American people any more in taxes; the bill would have offset the additional expenses by closing tax loopholes for hedge fund managers (you know, the guys who are barely scraping by on their multimillion dollar pay checks) and delaying implementation of a tax break for multinational corporations. Well, whenever anyone suggests making the rich pay for something, that's like waving a red cape in front of Sununu's face. Screw the kids if my donors can't upgrade their yachts this year!

But it's not just the little ones that Sununu has it in for. According to the New Hampshire Alliance for Retired Americans, Sununu voted 9 out of 10 times against senior citizens on issues that affect them.

To the rescue rides the former three-term governor of New Hampshire, Democrat *Jeanne Shaheen*. She was well-liked when she ran the state and had a record of increasing health coverage for uninsured children, expanding access to public kindergarten, and protecting women's reproductive rights. As governor of New Hampshire she signed a repeal of the state's law making abortion a felony. Jeanne Shaheen also understands one of the most pressing issues facing many young families: "The majority of parents work, and it's long past time our nation came to terms with this dynamic," Shaheen says. "We need to make quality child-care affordable and give parents the peace of mind that comes with knowing their children are safe."

When Jeanne Shaheen ran against Sununu in 2002, he narrowly defeated her for the Senate seat. All indications are that New Hampshire voters won't make the same mistake twice.

MINNESOTA

Al Franken

Poor Norm Coleman. He's the only person to benefit from the death of one of the most liberal members of the U.S. Senate. When Sen. Paul Wellstone's plane went down while he was campaigning only weeks before the 2002 election, Coleman and the right-wing pundits mocked Wellstone's funeral and, remarkably, rode that mean-spiritedness all the way to victory. Coleman is a Bush flunky through and through, voting with W. 90 percent of the time and staunchly supporting the Iraq War.

Presented now with a chance to redeem themselves—and to prove once again that Minnesotans have a great sense of humor (this *is* the state that elected a professional wrestler as governor in the '90s)—the voters of Minnesota can elect the Democrat *Al Franken* as their new senator come November. Not many Senate candidates can list *Saturday Night Live* on their résumés, but Franken brings a lot more than sharp satirical skills to the political table. He's a policy wonk, he does his homework, and his agenda includes climate-change legislation, universal healthcare, and withdrawing troops from Iraq. He's also a wrestler. A real one. In high school in Hopkins, Minnesota, he was on his varsity wrestling team, and 35 years later he still had the moves to put a heckler at a Dean rally in a wrestling hold. Imagine Franken in the Senate. It's just too cool, isn't it? Each day can begin with the Pledge, a prayer, and a bit of stand-up from Al. If any Republicans get out of line, Al can put them in a half nelson. Will the state that gave us Bob Dylan, the Coen Brothers, and Garrison Keillor please send Al Franken to the Senate? I think it's finally time for the Al Franken Decade.

OREGON

Jeff Merkley

Voters in Oregon used to elect Republicans who were to the left of most Democrats. Back in 1964, Oregon Senator Wayne Morse cast one of the two votes against the Gulf of Tonkin Resolution, which sent the U.S. whole-hog into Vietnam. Sen. Mark Hatfield was another strong anti-war senator from Oregon who voted against the first Gulf War in Kuwait and Iraq.

But there is still one relic in the Senate from the Pacific Northwest, Oregon Senator Gordon Smith. Forgetting to retire this year like Allard and Domenici, Smith is running for re-election. And why not, when the oil and gas industry have kicked nearly $300,000 to you? Smith made his own fortune in that great American contribution to the world of fine cuisine—frozen food. His company, Smith Frozen Foods, has been fined by the DEQ at least three times for illegally discharging polluted wastewater into nearby waterways. Facing possible defeat in 2008, Smith has had an election year epiphany on climate change, announcing his support for capping greenhouse gas emissions—after twice voting against similar bills.

Let's hope the brains of Oregonians aren't filled with too many frozen peas come November. Because there is an excellent alternative to Gordon Smith on the ballot: Democratic challenger *Jeff Merkley*. Currently serving as the Speaker of the Oregon House of Representatives, Merkley has taken Oregon down one of the most progressive paths in the nation. The Eugene *Register-Guard* described the 2007 session of the Oregon House under Merkley's leadership as "the most productive in recent memory, with important achievements in the areas of education funding, civil rights, consumer protection and budgetary stability." Merkley opposes the war, supports universal healthcare, and will take action to combat global warming. He will be a huge addition to improving things in the U.S. Senate.

MAINE

Tom Allen

It's tough to have to say goodbye to a Republican we like a lot of the time. But, as when we had to bid farewell to liberal Republican Sen. Lincoln Chafee of Rhode Island in 2006 (because in the end, it is all about which party can get 60 votes), we will have to bid a gracious adieu to Senator Susan Collins of Maine in this election. Collins is considered by many colleagues on her side of the aisle to be a Republican in name only, as she is pro-choice, pro-stem cell research, and doesn't always make tax cuts her highest priority. Nonetheless, Senator Collins voted for the war in Iraq, and as we said with Hillary, that's the deal-breaker.

Her Democratic opponent is Congressman *Tom Allen*. This 12-year veteran of the House of Representatives is in tune with the independent values of the people in this border state. The League of Conservation Voters and the Defenders of the Wildlife Action Fund both gave Allen top ratings. Allen has worked to reduce prescription drug prices for seniors and supports withdrawing troops from Iraq. He has introduced a number of bills intended to make healthcare more affordable for individuals and businesses, including the Small Business Health Plans Act, the Enhanced Healthcare for All Act, and the Long-Term Quality Care and Modernization Act. As a member of the House, he authored a bill banning the export of mercury. He voted against giving U.S. spy agencies expanded eavesdropping power and opposed President Bush's troop build-up in Iraq.

ALASKA

Mark Begich

There is no greater need to remove someone from our U.S. Senate than the Republican senator from Alaska, Sen. Ted Stevens. He's the longest-serving Republican in Senate history. That alone should be grounds for sending him back to the North Pole. If you remember, Stevens is the senator who tried to push through the federal pork funding for his "bridge to nowhere" in Alaska. He's a rabid right-winger and so that can mean only one thing. No, he has not been arrested in an airport restroom. Rather, the FBI is investigating him for corruption charges in a scandal involving an oil company. This influence peddling case has already seen the conviction of several Alaskan businessmen and state officials.

Stevens' Democratic challenger is the five-term mayor of Anchorage, *Mark Begich*. Not under investigation for anything, not wanting to build a bridge to Juneau, Begich is strongly opposed to Bush's No Child Left Behind education policy—calling it a "disaster in Alaska"—and supports an education policy that brings control of schools back to local communities. Begich is also a staunch defender of his constituents' civil liberties and promises to work to remedy the encroachments on Alaskans' constitutional rights, citing everything from "warrantless wiretapping, to the assault on habeas corpus, to the pursuit of REAL ID cards and retroactive immunity for telecom companies that illegally helped the federal government spy on innocent Americans."

MISSISSIPPI

Ronnie Musgrove

Woo-wee, it's special election time in Mississippi! Thanks to Trent Lott, who resigned in 2007. (The first rat off the sinking ship is usually the one with the best hairpiece. Lott couldn't simply wait for the election a year later to retire, he wanted out quick.)

The Republican governor of Mississippi appointed Rep. Roger Wicker to the Senate after Trent Lott cut and ran. It hasn't taken Wicker long to establish that he puts the interests of businesses before those of American workers. Representing a state in which women make only 73 cents for every dollar earned by men (lower than the national average), Roger Wicker voted against legislation that would have clearly established the rights of employees, including women and minorities, to

sue their employers for wage discrimination under existing anti-discrimination laws. Perhaps Wicker believes women should be happy that men let them work outside of the home. As a Congressman, Wicker also opposed decreasing the interest rate on student loans from 6.4 percent to 3.4 percent over a five-year period while at the same time voting against an effort to repeal 2004 tax cuts for oil companies.

Nonetheless, as Wicker has not been elected by the people, he must now stand for election in November. And he has to face no less than the popular former Democratic governor of Mississippi, *Ronnie Musgrove*. While governor, Musgrove managed to balance Mississippi's budget and at the same time increase education funding—no easy feat in perhaps the poorest state in the nation. Every child in Mississippi can thank former Governor Musgrove for putting an Internet connection in his or her classroom. He has a proven track record of bringing jobs to Mississippi and keeping a tight rein on government spending—something Republicans say they do but don't.

Is it possible for Mississippi to send a Democrat to the U.S. Senate? Perhaps this year anything can happen.

NORTH CAROLINA

Kay Hagan

People seem to like Sen. Elizabeth Dole (R-NC). I prefer to think of it as pity. After all she's got a guy who's hooked on Viagra chasing her every night. Just as she reached an age where she could relax at night, enjoy a nice bath, a glass of wine, and a good book, she and millions of other older women in the world now have husbands with four-hour erections wanting some immediate attention. Is this fair? Haven't they done enough—raising the kids, keeping the home together, balancing the checkbook, picking up after everybody and their friggin' mess? Just when they reach an age when they're trying to get a little peace and quiet—and yes, still have a roll in the hay every now and then—along comes a little pill that has Old Bob still going strong at 3am. "C'mon, Lizzie—one more time! I'm Bob Dole, dammit!"

When she isn't beating back an out-of-control wanker, Senator Elizabeth Dole has been voting with George W. Bush 92 percent of the time! That alone should be reason enough for her removal. What's it going to take, North Carolina?

How 'bout Democratic challenger *Kay Hagan*?

As a state senator for 9 years, Kay Hagan has created innovative tools for economic development, invested in technology and infrastructure to help develop the next century's medicine and jobs, passed some of the nation's toughest predatory lending laws, and supported education funding at all levels. She'd be an excellent replacement for Elizabeth Dole. As a going away gift, someone should get Mrs. Dole a ten-foot pole.

OKLAHOMA

Andrew Rice

There is no delicate way to describe the insanity that lives inside the mind of the Republican incumbent from Oklahoma, James M. Inhofe. With one hand he makes a fist and loudly proclaims that global warming is not caused by humans. With the other hand he accepts hundreds of thousands of dollars from the oil and gas industry. His views on marriage, sexuality, and education are equally antediluvian. He once boasted before the Senate, "I'm really proud to say that in the recorded history of our family, we've never had a divorce or any kind of homosexual relationship." Isn't that nice!

Inhofe's Democratic challenger is *Andrew Rice*.

Rice committed his life to public service after his brother died in the World Trade Center attacks. He has been a state senator since 2005, and during that time he voted in support of the poor and championed legislation for children and the uninsured. Rice has worked for the Texas Freedom Network, a nonprofit organization focused on countering the influence of the religious right on public policy decisions, and he founded the Progressive Alliance, an Oklahoma outfit dedicated to advancing "progressive, fair-minded and constitutional solutions to public policy problems." He has also tried his hand at documentary filmmaking, creating a film focused on the AIDS pandemic in India.

KENTUCKY

Bruce Lunsford

Shortly after businessman *Bruce Lunsford* won the Democratic nomination, polling showed him only 5 points behind the Senate's highest ranking Republican—none other than Mitch McConnell. Clearly, the Bluegrass state is seeing red about McConnell's record.

As Minority Leader, McConnell has worked tirelessly in defense of President Bush's Iraq War policy and the status quo, voting with Bush and the GOP approximately 95 percent of the time. And why shouldn't he? In an interview on *Face the Nation* in 2007, Senator McConnell called himself "the strongest supporter of the president you could find in the Senate." Yet while he supports Bush's plan of keeping soldiers in Iraq, McConnell doesn't seem to want to offer them much in the way of gratitude when they return home. He has voted against the 21st Century GI bill, which increases college funding for our service men and women, and he twice voted against increasing healthcare funding for veterans.

Vying for McConnell's seat is Bruce Lunsford, a businessman and former Commerce Secretary for the state of Kentucky. Lunsford promises to work to expand the State Children's Health Insurance Program (SCHIP) to cover *all* children (McConnell has opposed expanding the program's coverage). He also pledges to overhaul Bush's No Child Left Behind education policy, saying he will "oppose all attempts to privatize Social Security, fight to guarantee that corporations make good on their pension promises to workers, and push to lower prescription drug prices."

That's it for the United States Senate. Easy, huh? Not really. This effort is going to take each one of us. But it can be done.

Thirty House Seats We Can Win

Three long-held Republican congressional seats. Three special elections. Three stunning losses to the Democrats. That's what's *already happened* in 2008, and it is an omen of good things to come.

Republicans started worrying in early March, when physicist and Democrat Bill Foster beat out Republican dairyman Jim Oberweis in what was thought to have been a Republican stronghold in Illinois. The seat, vacated by former GOP House Speaker Dennis Hastert, had been in Republican hands for 20 years. Foster, who took 53 percent of the vote, even won the majority of the votes in parts of the district that essentially never vote for a Democrat. The district re-elected Hastert in 2006 with 60 percent of the vote, and gave Bush 55 percent of the vote in 2004. The reversal is nothing short of stunning.

Foster ran his campaign on a few key issues, including withdrawing from Iraq, tax breaks for the middle class, and enacting a system of universal healthcare. He also was clearly running a campaign of change with regard to how the Bush administration has handled issues of national security, arguing against giving immunity to telephone companies that spied on American citizens and against warrantless wiretapping.

Oberweis trotted out a traditional GOP platform of less government and more tax breaks, as well as the hot-button issue of illegal immigration. But it wasn't hot-button enough to persuade voters.

Two months later Republicans witnessed another fissure open up in their formerly rock-solid base. In a Louisiana district that includes Baton Rouge and hadn't sent a Democrat to the Capitol since 1974, Don Cazayoux pulled off an upset over Republican challenger Woody Jenkins. The seat had been held by 20-year-incumbent Richard Baker, who jumped ship for K Street. Dems didn't even bother to field a challenger for Baker in 2006.

Cazayoux is pro-gun and anti-abortion, which seems to be the minimum criteria for any Democratic candidate hoping to win in the Deep South. Although he's a social conservative, Cazayoux toes the Party lines when it comes to education and healthcare. Republicans tried to paint Cazayouz as a tax-happy liberal and linked him to Obama in television ads. But the Southern electorate seems to be wising up to GOP scare tactics.

The final, and perhaps biggest, blow in this Democratic trifecta came when Mississippi's Travis Childers won a seat vacated by Republican Roger Wicker, who had held the seat since 1995, defeating Greg Davis by 8 percentage points. Bush won 62 percent of the vote in the district in 2004. Childers, a social conservative, is anti-abortion. So was his Republican opponent. Childers is a staunch supporter of gun rights. So was Davis. So what was the difference between the two candidates? Childers opposed the war in Iraq. Davis supported it.

Republicans spent nearly a million dollars on ads tying Childers to Obama and even to Obama's former pastor, the Rev. Jeremiah Wright, but the plan seems to have backfired, as it appeared to bring out more black voters than usual. And those votes went Childers' way. Heck, they even called on their knight in shining armor, Vice President Dick Cheney, to ride into town and give his blessing to Davis. And when things started looking really desperate, they pulled out the nuclear option: First Lady Laura Bush. Not even the former librarian, in a recorded message sent to voters throughout the district, could woo enough Mississippians to vote for Davis.

What happened? According to Jack Bass, who has written extensively on Southern politics, the Democratic victories in the two traditional Republican strongholds in the South "suggest a region in transformation, with dynamic economic growth, an expanded black middle class, the arrival of millions of white migrants, the return of scores of thousands of African-American expatriates, and an emerging native white generation with little or no memory of racial segregation." Or, more to the point, it suggests BIG TROUBLE for the Republicans, who have for too long relied on racism and religious extremism in the Deep South and elsewhere.

What do Republicans have to say about their situation? Let's listen in:

Rep. Tom Davis wrote a 20-page memo to his Republican colleagues saying that "the Republican brand is in the trash can . . . if we were dog food, they would take us off the shelf."

Former Speaker of the House Newt Gingrich: "The Republican brand has been so badly damaged that if Republicans try to run an anti-Obama, anti-Rev. Wright . . . campaign, they are simply going to fail," Gingrich said. "This model has already been tested with disastrous results."

And: "Either congressional Republicans are going to chart a bold course of real change or they are going to suffer decisive losses this November."

Suffer might be too polite a word. There's the potential here for a political bloodbath. Here's a look at 30 House seats we could possibly win— if we do the work that needs to be done . . .

ALABAMA'S 2ND DISTRICT

Bobby Bright

State Rep. Jay Love is on his way to winning the Republican nomination for Terry Everett's open seat after a primary battle with State Senator Harri Anne Smith. Before entering politics, Love made his fortune by operating 16 Subway Sandwich franchises, opening his first shop in 1992. He's now pumped at least $500,000 of his sandwich money into this primary race. Among his legislative accomplishments was the sponsoring of the Unborn Victims of Violence Act and a bill to prevent kids from being exposed to violent or sexually explicit videogames.

Popular Montgomery Mayor *Bobby Bright* is the Democrat running in this district with a 29 percent African-American population. He stands a good chance of snatching yet another "safe" seat away from the Republicans. Bright considers himself a "social conservative," who's "pro-life, pro-gun" and "strong on military." Well, okay, it's Alabama. Chalk up one sure win for the Dems.

ALASKA'S LONE
CONGRESSIONAL DISTRICT

Ethan Berkowitz

The Alaska Republican corruption racket is finally going out of business. Senator Ted Stevens and 18-term Republican Representative Don Young are both tainted by a federal corruption investigation, so Alaska Republicans are scrambling to hold on to their long-held seats in Washington. There has even been some infighting among the GOP, as Lieutenant Governor Sean Parnell shocked the party by announcing his candidacy for Young's seat. The primary takes place after this book is published, and polls showed Parnell and Young in a statistical dead heat.

In addition to the FBI corruption investigation, Alaska's lone representative to the U.S. House is under scrutiny by the Justice Department for changing the wording of a $10-million earmark in a 2005 transportation bill—*after* the bill had already been approved by both houses of Congress but before the President signed it into law. The edit benefited a major donor to Young's campaign.

The way things look like right now, all Republican challenger Sean Parnell has to do is show up at the congressional primary and he'll beat the scandal-tainted Young. Parnell is currently serving as Lt. Gov., is a lawyer, and is a staunch social conservative who wants to leave healthcare in the hands of "the market" (translation: apply a little mascara, rouge, and lipstick to our moribund system).

The Democrats are resting their hopes on former state House Minority Leader *Ethan Berkowitz* (he of the famed Fairbanks Berkowitzes, not the lesser-known Nome Berkowitzes). He supports withdrawing the troops from Iraq, saying that "our continued presence [there] isn't making us any safer." Unlike most Democrats, but in line with his Alaskan constituents, he supports drilling in ANWR.

ARIZONA'S 1st DISTRICT

The Republicans are trying to hold on to a seat vacated by Rep. Rick Renzi, who faces 35 counts of corruption in federal courts. The party's top recruit to succeed Renzi

Ann Kirkpatrick decided to quit the race early, so Republicans have been desperate to find a good candidate to replace the ethically-challenged Renzi.

Sydney Hay is the likely Republican candidate. Hay, a former conservative talk radio host, is the president of the Arizona Mining Association. She says she was "inspired by the Reagan revolution" and is "concerned about the coarsening culture in America." She opposes a woman's right to an abortion and supports school voucher programs. Her proposal for addressing the nation's healthcare crisis is straight out of the health insurance industry's play book—encouraging investment in health saving accounts, reducing the ability of lawyers to sue, and encouraging healthcare "consumers" to "shop around."

Democratic candidate *Ann Kirkpatrick* is a former State Representative and has the support of popular Democratic Governor Janet Napolitano. After earning a law degree, Kirkpatrick became the first female Deputy County Attorney of Coconino County and later became City Attorney of Sedona. She's a mother, has served her community as a legislator, teacher, and a member of many local organizations such as the United Way of Northern Arizona and the Board of Directors of Big Sisters. Emily's List quotes her as saying that

"Washington needs to start working for people again and focus on what really matters—like preserving our open spaces and way of life, while creating jobs, restoring fiscal responsibility, and improving our schools." She calls the war in Iraq a "disaster" and says we must make it a top priority to end our involvement in it. She has worked for equal pay for women and minorities, and the Sierra Club has given her an A for her environmental record. She doesn't run a mining association, but my guess is Ann Kirkpatrick would strip-mine Congress of its BS if she were elected.

CALIFORNIA'S 4TH DISTRICT

Charlie Brown

Republican candidate Tom McClintock has been involved in California politics for several years. He's currently a State Senator and has made losing bids in the 2003 gubernatorial recall election and the 2006 lieutenant governor campaign. He loves capitalism and wants the rich to keep their money while the country goes broke. His love of money has led him to take advantage of a tax-free per diem entitled to California legislators who live more than 50 miles from the capital.

The problem is, McClintock lives only 14 miles from the capital. During his years in elected office in California he's raked in $306,000 in per diem money.

The issues McClintock is most heavily involved in are economic and tax policies, where he is a "Club for Growth"-certified conservative. He receives A ratings from all of California's big business, antitax interest groups as well as straight A's from the California Republican Assembly, who support candidates with "unwavering Republican principles." He promises to support making the Bush tax cuts for the rich permanent and "reduce the size of the federal government."

Democratic candidate *Charlie Brown* is a 26-year veteran of the U.S. Air Force and a 22-year member of the Sierra Club. He opposed the Iraq war from the beginning and came close to winning this seat in the 2006 elections. With the retirement of Republican Rep. Doolittle (who is under investigation for his ties to imprisoned lobbyist Jack Abramoff) and a big year for Democrats approaching, he's in a good position to take this seat for the Democrats.

After a career serving in the Air Force, the country's continued involvement in the Iraq war has inspired Brown to run for office. Before the war began, he didn't believe there were any WMD and did not support the invasion. He also wants Congress to implement the recommendations of the 9/11 Commission. Domestically, he supports a ban on members of Congress becoming lobbyists within 5 years of leaving office. He also supports allowing the federal government to negotiate with pharmaceutical companies to bring down the cost of prescription drugs for Medicare recipients. He's against Social Security privatization and supports raising the income cap on Social Security to help make it sustainable.

COLORADO'S 4TH DISTRICT

Betsy Markey

Winning with the slimmest margin of any candidate in 2006, the Democrats see Republican Marilyn Musgrave's seat as prime for the picking. Musgrave is notorious for using divisive social issues to boost conservative turnout, and she's doing it again this election cycle. She supports a state ballot measure on "personhood" that would define a person as "any human being from the moment of fertilization." It's the first ballot measure of this kind in the country, but if it helps the desperate Republican Party hold on to seats in November, you can bet your Rocky Mountain high that other states will give it a go.

She was on *Rolling Stone*'s list of the 10 worst members of Congress because of her career focus on "regulating the bedroom behavior of her fellow Americans." This includes running for school board on a platform of eliminating sex education; she was able to achieve "abstinence only" programs with sex-related passages scrubbed from health textbooks. In the U.S. Congress, she's proposed a constitutional amendment to ban gay marriage, calling it "the most important issue that we face today."

Challenging a seat that has been held by the Republicans since 1973 is Democrat *Betsy Markey*. She is a former aide to Colorado Senator Ken Salazar and a former State Department official, as well as a businesswoman. She counts healthcare and education as two of the most important issues facing America and has the backing of Emily's List. Her economic plan also includes something we don't hear people propose or mention too often—cutting government spending by cutting the federal government's PR contracts by 10 percent. This includes no-bid contracts given to the likes of conservative commentator Armstrong Williams, who was given tax dollars to promote No Child Left Behind in his newspaper columns and his pundit stints on cable TV.

CONNECTICUT'S
4TH DISTRICT

Jim Himes

Christopher Shays is a rare bird: a Republican congressman in New England. In the 2006 elections, the species nearly went extinct, with Shays—who supported the war in Iraq—the lone survivor. With Obama topping the Democratic ticket and voter registration on the rise, the Democrats have an opportunity to remove the term "New England House Republicans" from the political lexicon.

When it comes to issues that will lead to Shays' exit from Congress, the first three that come to mind are Iraq, Iraq, and Iraq. He voted and vouched for the war and the Bush-Cheney Middle East policies. Five years after voting for the war, Shays admitted that he had yet to read the pre-war National Intelligence Estimate of 2002. He has openly stated that "I've been carrying the bucket when it comes to the war," but representing a liberal district in Connecticut, he's about to kick that bucket. And in a strange, creepy (and what I hope is a) coincidence, like Joe Lieberman at a previous State of the Union Address, Shays was caught on camera exchanging a kiss with the goofy-sounding guy who'd just stumbled his way through the speech. A changing position on Iraq is too little and too late to overcome his kiss of political death.

Democratic candidate *Jim Himes* was born in Lima, Peru, and moved to the United States at the age of 10. He went to Harvard and won a Rhodes scholarship to study at Oxford. For the past few years, Himes has been an executive at a non-profit organization that addresses urban poverty by helping low-income families with tax preparation and financial assistance, funding affordable housing in the Northeast, and using green technology to lower energy costs. He wants to bring these types of solutions to government in Washington.

FLORIDA'S 24TH DISTRICT

Suzanne Kosmas

Republican incumbent Tom Feeney is also from the Jack Abramoff-wing of the Republican Party. In 2003, he took a trip to Scotland with the imprisoned former lobbyist and poster boy for the Washington culture of corruption. This is the same golf junket that led to Rep. Bob Ney being jailed on corruption charges. Feeney may avoid doing hard time, but he should start looking for another job.

He's voted against withdrawal from Iraq and in favor of funding the war with no strings attached. He's also voted for the FISA domestic spying bill to give the government more power to eavesdrop without a court order, and voted against SCHIP, the state children's healthcare fund. Feeney is a reliable Republican vote, having sided with the GOP over 90 percent of the time.

Democratic opponent *Suzanne Kosmas* has served in the Florida House of Representatives and on local boards of the United Way Women's Initiative, the Atlantic Center for the Arts, Southeast Volusia Habitat for Humanity, and Volusia County's Cultural Arts Advisory Board. She helped create the first local "Women Build" program with the United Way and Habitat for Humanity, which recruits female volunteers to build affordable housing for single mothers. She has the backing of many labor unions and Emily's List.

ILLINOIS' 10TH DISTRICT

Dan Seals

In 2005, Democrat-turned-Republican Mark Kirk said he was "OK with discrimination against young Arab males from terrorist-producing states." He was immediately criticized by State Senator Barack Obama and Rep. Jan Schakowsky but stood by his comments. This is one guy the Democrats weren't sad to lose. The incumbent Republican candidate has also been a war-enabling obstructionist, voting against the withdrawal of troops from Iraq and in favor of funding the war with no strings attached. In a vote to allow the federal government to directly negotiate with drugmakers to lower Medicare prescription drug costs, the Democrats voted in favor, the Republicans voted against, and facing re-election, Kirk was a no-show; he didn't vote.

Democratic candidate *Daniel J. Seals* hopes to be part of a rising tide—led by Barack Obama—

sweeping Democrats into office in Illinois. He's aggressively going after his opponent for supporting the Bush administration, making false claims of "independence," and failing to keep the price of gas in check. He also calls healthcare a "moral issue" and says that the government should "develop a national program of health insurance that provides a basic level of healthcare that is portable and affordable." A future co-sponsor of Rep. Conyers' HR 676?

ILLINOIS' 11TH DISTRICT

Debbie
Halvorson

Republican Rep. Jerry Weller is retiring, so the cash-strapped Illinois GOP is looking to ready-mix concrete magnate Martin Ozinga III to fund his own campaign for the open seat. He did a four-hour stint manning the pumps at a local gas station in June of '08 to promote his "energy policy." It was a perfect setting for a man whose less-than-innovative energy proposals include drilling the crap out of everything in sight in search of oil, building more refineries, and doing away with the Illinois state gas tax. He calls alternative energy a "second energy priority."

All of this nonsense should hopefully make it smooth sailing for Ozinga's opponent, Democratic candidate *Debbie Halvorson*. Halvorson is the first woman to be elected Majority Leader in Illinois and has been in the state Senate for 10 years. She was a leader in the effort to get low-cost prescription drugs to Illinois seniors and disabled individuals and has been called "arguably among the most powerful women in Illinois." She told Emily's List that "Our district has been underserved for too long, and I want to provide real leadership on the issues that matter to Illinois families." Halvorson supports tax cuts for middle- and low-income families, she's for closing the wage gap between the rich and the poor, and supports providing affordable, quality child care and healthcare for America's working families.

LOUISIANA'S 4TH DISTRICT

Paul Carmouche

Republican Jim McCrery has represented the district since 1989 and is one of nearly 30 retiring House Republicans to jump off a sinking ship. He has endorsed unknown attorney Jeff Thompson in the Republican primary. Thompson himself faces a primary challenge from two other unknown Republicans. Among Thompson's key plans are increasing our military might and expanding oil exploration and refining capacity at home. The same old same old in a year when people want *change*.

The Democrats are likely to nominate *Paul Carmouche*, a respected local prosecutor, to fill McCrery's seat. The district has a 33 percent black population, and it's near districts in which Democrats have won surprising special election victories in the south. Carmouche says he will "fight for Louisiana's working families and work to provide better healthcare for our veterans and reservists, give our middle-class families the tax relief they need, and stand up for Louisiana's values in Washington." Like the value of a good levee or two.

MICHIGAN'S 7TH DISTRICT

Mark Schauer

Republican Tim Walberg's stay in the U.S. House of Representatives will be a short one. He is a freshman member who won his 2006 race with less than 50 percent of the vote. During his short stint in Congress, he has been one of Bush and Cheney's biggest cheerleaders on Iraq, claiming that soldiers are telling him that Iraq is as safe as Detroit or Chicago. He said on a radio show in 2007, "80 to 85 percent . . . of the country is reasonably under control, at least as well as Detroit or Chicago or any of our other big cities." Adding, "in many places it's as safe and cared for as Detroit or Harvey, Ill., or some other places that have trouble with armed violence that takes place on occasion." He also invited Dick Cheney to Michigan where they held a private fundraiser that raked in more than $100,000. Walberg is anti-abortion and opposes embryonic stem cell research. The Michigan League of Conservation Voters (MLCV) gave Walberg 5 points out of a possible 100 for his record on environmental issues in 2007. Of the 20 issues the MLCV tracked, Walberg voted in support of only one and against 19 pro-environmental measures, including tax subsidies to encourage the development of clean, renewable energy sources; setting higher fuel efficiency standards; and providing financing for water infrastructure projects.

Democrats have nominated *Mark Schauer* for Walberg's seat. Schauer is the leader of the Democrats in the Michigan State Senate and has spent his career working and serving Michigan. He was a Battle Creek city commissioner and executive director of the Community Action Agency of South Central Michigan. Making Michigan's wobbly economy a priority, Schauer says he'll join Senators Levin and Stabenow to change our federal trade policies to help bring jobs back to Michigan. He has also voted to increase the minimum wage and protect the earned income tax credit.

MICHIGAN'S 9TH DISTRICT

Gary Peters

Eight-term Republican congressman Joe Knollenberg won a close race in 2006 despite heavily outspending his opponent. With the tide turning blue, what used to be a safe seat for Republicans is now up for grabs, and Knollenberg and his staff are starting to feel the heat. Knollenberg, who's been a rubber stamp for the Bush administration, got some national attention when his chief-of-staff, Trent Wisecup, had a wild-eyed meltdown in front of a community activist who had asked Rep. Knollenberg about his policies on the war and why he voted against increasing funding for

SCHIP, the popular children's health insurance program. Wisecup called the constituent "anti-American," and "pro-Toyota," and said he was "against the country," and wanted "Iran to win." Sounds a lot like the Republican party platform—let's give this guy a primetime slot at the Convention! To view a video clip of the diatribe, go to www.retirejoeknollenberg.com.

Democratic candidate *Gary Peters* was a Lieutenant Commander in the U.S. Navy Reserve, a city councilman, and was appointed by the governor as Michigan's Lottery Commissioner. He's running hard against the Bush administration's policies and Rep. Knollenberg, who supports them. He has the support of General Wesley Clark and VoteVets.org.

During his time in the Michigan State Senate, he authored a bill to ban drilling for oil and gas under the Great Lakes. He was also a founder and co-chair of the Senate Arts Caucus to promote culture, art and creativity in Michigan.

MINNESOTA'S 3RD DISTRICT

Ashwin Madia

Republican Erik Paulsen is a state representative and a former staffer to the retiring Rep. Ramstad, who has held this seat since 1991. Dick Cheney held a private fundraiser in Minnesota in June that some local Republicans didn't attend because they want nothing to do with him; Paulsen's spokesperson admitted, "Paulsen did stop by the event." Even though Paulsen was willing to attend a fundraiser with Dick Cheney to help raise funds for his campaign, he's not as willing to talk about Mr. Cheney's most controversial policy—the Iraq War. A search of Paulsen's website—from "Issues" to "About Erik" to "The Paulsen Record," and even using his website's search engine, turned up no hits for the word "Iraq."

His opponent, Democratic challenger *Ashwin Madia*, served in Iraq and isn't afraid to use that four-letter word.

Madia's parents came to the United States from India with $19 in their pockets. Their son Ashwin, born in Boston, went on to attend University of Minnesota and New York University Law School. He joined the Marines and is one of many Iraq war veterans running for office in the Democratic Party in the hopes of ending the war before another 4,000 soldiers perish.

After his time serving in Baghdad, Madia is now calling for a withdrawal of troops from Iraq over a period of 18 to 24 months.

MISSOURI'S 6TH DISTRICT

Kay Barnes

Republican incumbent Sam Graves needs to come out of the closet—the *congressional closet. Roll Call*, the inside-the-beltway newspaper, has noted that Graves' TV ads state everything about him *except* that he's the incumbent in this race and that he's a Republican. Though he has represented this district since 2001, he's too ashamed to admit that he's a member of Congress and the Republican Party in his own paid advertisements! I sympathize with the guy, but I don't think he'll fool the people of the sixth district of Missouri again. This is a swing district that gets attention from both national parties, and one of Graves' funding sources has been the disgraced former Representative Tom DeLay's political action committee.

Even though he's a closet-Republican and closet-Congressman, he's voted with his fellow Republicans 91 percent of the time in the current Congress. He's even in a dwindling group of Republicans who are still publicly claiming that China is drilling for oil off American shores near Cuba. In an effort to drum up support for offshore drilling, Republicans have falsely claimed that China is currently drilling for oil near Cuba. Dick Cheney went so far as to invoke the Red Menace to drive his point home: "'Even the communists have figured out that a good answer to high prices is more supply. Yet Congress has said . . . no to drilling off Florida." In an unprecedented move, after being corrected by many sources, Dick Cheney admitted that he was mistaken when he said this (and said that conservative columnist George Will was his source for this false info. Yes, they have begun to eat their own.). Republican Senator Mel Martinez went on the Senate floor and corrected the record saying that the China-Cuba oil drilling story was not true. After both Martinez and even Dick Cheney's corrections, Sam Graves continues to use the fake China-Cuba drilling story to push for more offshore drilling. Hey, Sam—I heard bin Laden and the Boogeyman are drilling in Cuba, too!

In 1999 Democratic candidate *Kay Barnes* became the first female mayor of Kansas City, the largest city in Missouri, where she served two terms. She is currently a Distinguished Professor for Public Leadership at Park University and holds Master's Degrees in secondary education and public administration. She also ran her own small business, a human resource development firm, and has served the community as the first coordinator of the Women's Resource Center at the University of Missouri—Kansas City and as a staff member of Kansas City's Metropolitan Inter-Church Agency.

On the environment, Barnes believes the U.S. should have signed the Kyoto Protocol and gone even further to raise the environmental standard and lead the world on this issue. She's also a potential supporter of Rep. Conyers' HR 676—she says she's dedicated to universal healthcare and is "willing to consider all options to provide real health security" and that "we must look at every option before choosing the one that best fits our economy."

Oh, and she's a first cousin of Walter Cronkite. What more do you need, Missouri?

NEW JERSEY'S 3RD DISTRICT

John Adler

You know, one thing I've always said is that we need more defense contractors and war profiteers in Congress. Leave it to the great state of New Jersey to give us Chris Myers, the Republican candidate gunning for the seat being vacated by Jim Saxon. Myers is a vice president of defense contractor Lockheed Martin. Atop his list of accomplishments at Lockheed, Myers specialized in developing more efficient, effective and innovative tools for killing people, such as advanced sensors and weapons systems for the U.S. Navy.

Earlier in his tenure at the defense contractor, Myers served as vice president of Sea-Based Missile Defense. Isn't it ironic that someone whose career has been in sea-based defense is now trying to board the Titanic known as House Republican minority?

It is no surprise that this Lockheed executive/Republican candidate for Congress called on the Senate to pass the FISA intelligence bill that will give the President more power to spy on Americans and give telecom companies immunity for their role in enabling government spying. He is also calling on the Bush tax cuts for the rich to remain permanent.

Unlike many House Republicans, Myers is NOT in favor of building walls along the border to prevent illegal immigration. He thinks it won't be effective and instead believes in high-tech solutions such as . . . sensors and cameras purchased from Lockheed Martin! Lockheed submitted a bid to the Department of Homeland Security to build a "virtual border fence" in 2006 and continues to push for the high-tech solutions to these problems. With Chris Myers, Lockheed Martin will have a trusted family member in Congress who can help deliver the bacon.

Attempting to stop Lockheed/Myers is Democratic candidate *John Adler*, a five-term State Senator in New Jersey where he was a key figure behind the state's Smoke Free Air Act, which banned smoking indoors and in the workplace and received broad bipartisan support. The Sierra Club has endorsed his campaign, and he recently called for an end to all federal subsidies to oil companies.

Adler is New Jersey's hope to stop the Myers missile from finding a home in Congress.

NEW JERSEY'S 7TH DISTRICT

Linda Stender

Leonard Lance is a longtime State Representative who won a nasty Republican primary against several opponents hoping to hold on to a longtime Republican seat vacated by Rep. Mike Ferguson. The Republican primary contests in New Jersey have been described as "bloodbaths," as politicians scramble to hold on to their seats against a strong political tide against them. Lance's top priority is to make sure the Bush administration's economic policies continue long after Mr. Bush is out of office. He wants to make his tax cuts for the rich permanent and repeal the Estate Tax (or so-called "Death Tax for the Rich"). The Bush economy hasn't been bad for everyone, and Mr. Lance seems to be one of the few who's better off than he was eight years ago.

Democratic candidate *Linda Stender* is a New Jersey Assemblywoman who has focused on the environment, global warming, and gas prices during her campaign. She sponsored New Jersey's "Global Warming Response Act." This was a major piece of legislation and only the third of its kind in the nation; it requires the state to cut emissions of global warming gases to 1990 levels by the year 2020 and reduce greenhouse gas emissions to 80 percent below 2006 levels by the year 2050. When Governor Corzine signed the bill into law last year, the ceremony drew national attention and included a speech by Al Gore, who said he's adding New Jersey's efforts to his famous global warming slideshow.

Stender previously served as Councilwoman and Mayor of Fanwood, New Jersey, and came within 3,000 votes of winning this House seat in 2006 against the incumbent. She has the support of Emily's List, Democracy for America, and the Sierra Club.

NEW MEXICO'S 1st DISTRICT

Martin Heinrich

Like John McCain, Republican Darren White has relied on George W. Bush to help raise money for his campaign to fill Heather Wilson's open seat, albeit at a closed-door event in order to avoid having voters actually see him associate with the man whom only 29 percent of the American support. Bush arrived in Albuquerque at 11:30 am, shook a few hands, posed for a few pictures with New Mexico's wealthiest Republicans, raised $300,000, and snuck over to Arizona at 2:30 pm to do the same for the McCain campaign. After the event, White promised that his campaign would be "shaking up Washington with strong, independent leadership."

White is the Bernalillo County Sheriff and has worked in law enforcement his entire career. He also served as county chairman for the Bush/Cheney campaign in 2004 and plans to continue their tax polices if elected to Congress.

Democratic challenger *Martin Heinrich* is a former Albuquerque City Councilor and was appointed by Governor Bill Richardson as Natural Resources Trustee for the State of New Mexico, where he worked on environmental issues. While on the city council, he helped raise the minimum wage in New Mexico to $7.50. But the issue most critical to him has been the environment. He's served on the boards of various environmental groups and is executive director of a non-profit group dedicated to environmental education. He has worked to preserve the Ojito Wilderness as well as land in the Rio Grande State Park. New Mexico is "The Land of Enchantment," and Heinrich wants to make sure future generations of New Mexicans get a chance to be enchanted, too.

NEVADA'S 3rd DISTRICT

Dina Titus

Republican Jon Porter has only been in Congress since 2002 and he's already gotten accustomed to the ways of Washington. A former staffer to Porter accused him of making fundraising phone calls from his congressional office, which is illegal (but the FBI chose not to investigate). And after visiting Iraq, he claimed that we had to stay longer because if we left, gas prices would go up to $9/gallon. Porter has voted along the Republican Party line 85 percent of the time during this congressional session. This includes votes in favor of war without end, in favor of war spending with no strings attached, and in favor of the FISA to expand the President's power to spy on Americans. He also voted against raising the federal minimum wage and against allowing the government to negotiate directly with drug makers to lower the cost of drugs in Medicare.

Democratic candidate *Dina Titus* has served in the Nevada Legislature since 1988, including a stint as the Democratic Leader. She's also taught American and Nevada Politics at UNLV and specializes in education policy. Her long career in the legislature has included major accomplishments such as sponsoring a bill creating Nevada's Check Up Program to cover uninsured children. She's also co-sponsored successful legislation allowing Nevadans to purchase cheaper prescription drugs from Canada and legislation to double penalties for those committing crimes against the disabled. Her long career for standing up for the less fortunate led to the 2006 dedication of the Dina Titus Estates, an affordable housing complex for the disabled that now bears her name because of all of her work over the years.

NEW YORK'S 13TH DISTRICT

Maybe the Republicans of Staten Island weren't meant to have this seat. First, their incumbent Vito Fossella had to drop out after being arrested for drunk driving and later admitting to having an extramarital affair and fathering a child out of wedlock. The Republicans scrambled to find a warm body to fill in for Fossella. They settled for Frank Powers,

Mike McMahon

a retired Wall Street executive who has worked as a behind-the-scenes Republican operative. In a sign of how little support Powers had, he didn't even have his entire family behind him. One of the two candidates vying for the Libertarian Party nomination to face Powers was . . . Fran Powers—Frank Powers' son. About his relationship with his father, Fran says, "I like my father. I just don't like that he's going to vote straight for the Republican ticket and support Republican causes. This seat is too important to be in the Republican Party's hands." Sadly, a month after Powers was picked to replace Fossella, he died from a heart attack at the age of 67. Once again, the Republicans are scrambling for a replacement.

Democratic candidate *Mike McMahon* is a City Councilman who has the backing of Rep. Charlie Rangel and other New York Democrats as they try to flip the last Republican district in New York City. On Iraq, McMahon says, "I am opposed to the Iraq War and the time to start bringing home our fighting men and women is now." In seeking to take over the seat held by scandal-plagued Vito Fossella, McMahon says that he wants to bring "integrity and respect back" to his district. The bar has been set so low by Fossella that it shouldn't be a problem; when asked if he, like Fossella, had ever driven drunk or had an extra-marital affair, McMahon answered "no" to both. Give this man a cigar! . . . Wait! No! . . . A cigar's a bad idea . . .

NEW YORK'S 25TH DISTRICT

Dan Maffei

Republican candidate Dale Sweet-land served in the Onondaga County Legislature from 1994 to 2007. He's running for Dan Walsh's seat in the House after losing a Republican primary for the Onondaga County Executive position. He describes himself as "fiercely pro-business." He's also backing the gas-tax holiday scheme John McCain has supported and that won't do anything to lower gas prices.

Syracuse native and Democrat *Dan Maffei* came within 3,400 votes in his race for this seat in 2006 despite running against better-funded opponent Dan Walsh. He railed against the war in Iraq and, despite lack of name recognition, almost pulled off the upset because of his campaign against the war. Walsh surprised New York Republicans by announcing he won't run again, and

Maffei is now in good position to take this seat for the Democrats. Maffei is pushing for a tax on oil companies' outrageous profits while his opponent is calling for the gimmick "gas tax holiday" that won't help anyone.

NEW YORK'S 26TH DISTRICT

Jon Powers

New York State Democrats are rallying behind Iraq war veteran *Jonathan Powers*, a former Army Captain looking to take the seat vacated by powerful Republican Tom Reynolds. Moved by the war's impact on the Iraqi people, Jon Powers returned home and founded a non-profit organization called War Kids Relief in Baghdad to help Iraqi children deal with the aftermath of war. Powers has the support of Vote Vets, Vet Pac, and many local labor unions. Captain Powers is an Eagle Scout, and is currently a high school social studies teacher. His opponent is Chris Lee, a wealthy Republican businessman who has the backing of the retiring Rep. Reynolds. His agenda is built entirely around cutting taxes and loosening government regulations or eliminating them altogether. He is not an Eagle Scout.

NEW YORK'S 29TH DISTRICT

Eric Massa

Republican incumbent Randy Kuhl has been a big supporter of the Bush/Cheney war and their foreign policy. He has welcomed both of them to fundraisers in his districts, and before the 2006 elections was one of the few Republican candidates to hold a public event with Cheney, who used the opportunity to blast Democrats who have spoken out against the war. If that wasn't bad enough, his divorce papers, leaked on the Internet, accused him of endangering his wife's mental and physical well-being, once threatening to shoot her with two shotguns at a dinner party they hosted. Finally, Kuhl was arrested and charged with a DUI in 1997 and refused to seek counseling for his alcohol abuse. You might say the guy has "issues."

Eric Massa is another military veteran running for Congress as a Democrat. He spent 24 years on active duty for the Navy, and his biggest assignment was as a special assistant to General Wesley Clark in Panama when Clark was NATO Supreme Allied Commander. Like Clark, Massa was against the Iraq war from the beginning, which is one of his reasons for getting involved in politics. He's also a cancer survivor who knows what it's like to "get sick, lose your job, and have bills you can't pay."

OHIO'S 15TH DISTRICT

Mary Jo Kilroy

Democrat *Mary Jo Kilroy* came within 1,062 votes of winning this seat in 2006. Her opponent then, Deborah Pryce, is now retiring after 8 terms, creating a great Democratic opportunity in the unfortunate bellwether state of Ohio. A county commissioner who is making the Iraq war one of her top issues, Kilroy says that "It's time to bring our troops home. It was a mistake to invade Iraq and it's a mistake to stay there now." While Kilroy served as County Commissioner, Franklin County was named one of the five best-managed counties in the country by *Governing Magazine*. While school board president in Columbus, she helped create the Columbus Franklin County Affordable Housing Trust Corporation to promote home ownership and increase minority home ownership. She also helped create Access Health Columbus to provide healthcare for uninsured and low-income families. She also helped implement the Quality

Contractor Policy which rewards or penalizes county contractors based on whether they pay their workers livable wages and with good benefits.

"Lobbyist" just might have replaced "liberal" as the dirtiest word in Washington, as evidenced by her opponent, Republican candidate Steve Stivers' clumsy attempts to dodge the label. While vice president of government relations at Banc One Ohio Corp. from 1995 to 2002, he was registered as a lobbyist with the Joint Legislative Ethics Committee. When asked about this on the campaign trail, Stivers spun himself in circles, claiming "I was never a lobbyist per se." After being pressed on the issue, he finally acknowledged that he was registered as a lobbyist, but then added, "it's interesting that everybody wants to talk about my past. I want to talk about the future." Funny, that's what most Republicans I've talked to have been saying this year.

Like John McCain, Stivers tries to portray himself as an independent-minded moderate, but his record in the Ohio State Senate hasn't always lived up to this. He voted against stem-cell research in a bill supported by Ohio Governor Ted Strickland. He's also earned a zero rating from the Ohio League of Conservation Voters and Naral

Pro-Choice Ohio, a 100 percent rating from the Ohio Chamber of Commerce.

NORTH CAROLINA'S
8TH DISTRICT

Larry Kissell

Of all the inane comments made about the Iraq War, those made by Republican incumbent Robin Hayes rank right near the top. According to the *Charlotte Observer*, to stabilize Iraq Hayes proposed "spreading the message of Jesus Christ, the message of peace on earth, good will towards men. Everything depends on everyone learning about the birth of the Savior." Maybe we should have thought of that *before* we started bombing the crap out of their country! During the 2004 election cycle, Hayes was the second largest recipient of campaign funds from the machine of Rep. Tom DeLay.

He's also been a reliable Republican, voting the party line 91 percent of the time. He skipped out on voting on the FISA surveillance bill, but has voted against withdrawal from Iraq, and in favor of no strings attached funding for the war. He voted for the war, the Bush tax cuts, and the extension of the Bush tax cuts. He voted against a ban on "cruel, inhuman and degrading treatment on detainees" held by American forces. And that's just the icing on the cake for his cruel, inhuman and degrading career in the United States Congress.

Larry Kissell came within 329 votes of defeating Rep. Hayes in 2006, and that was without much help from the national Democratic Party. After his strong showing and with the political winds blowing against the Republicans, this could definitely be another Democratic pickup. Kissell, a lifelong Democrat, is a social studies teacher and former textile worker. The top issue he's fought for has been for a quick end to the war in Iraq. Since 2006 he's said, "We staged our way into Iraq in one year, there's no reason we can't stage our way out in one year." He's also been endorsed by the North Carolina AFL-CIO and the North Carolina Association of Educators.

OHIO'S 1st DISTRICT

Steve Driehaus

Republican Steve Chabot has held this seat since 1992. Early in his career in Congress, Chabot would rail against pork-barrel spending and government waste, saying "I wasn't sent up here to bring pork back to my district." After more than a decade in Washington, Chabot has changed his tune. In an article titled, "Chabot aims earmarks at places linked to donors," *The Hill* notes that $1.6 million in earmarks in a 2007 appropriations bill were headed to organizations and projects linked to supporters and donors of Rep. Chabot. I wonder if it has anything to do with the upcoming election.

Chabot has been a reliable Republican vote in Congress—91 percent of the time he's been in line during this congressional session. He's voted in favor of the war. He voted against the State Children's Health Insurance Program, against repealing tax cuts to oil companies, in favor of extending the Bush tax cuts for the wealthy and against raising the minimum wage to a measly $7.25. Judging from his record, the only time he's voted in favor of the less fortunate, needy, or hard-pressed is on a bill that applied to only one American—Terri Schiavo. So if you're a citizen in Ohio's first congressional district, the only way your congressman will show any compassion and fight for your healthcare (or Social Security or jobs or affordable housing or anything else) is if *you're in a permanent vegetative state*!

Democratic candidate *Steve Driehaus* was elected in 2000 as a State Representative and was named "Rookie of the Year" and "Legislator of the Year" by the *Cincinnati Enquirer* and the Ohio Association of Election Officials. He volunteered in the Peace Corps and served in Senegal. Sadly, he's an anti-abortion Democrat, but he has the backing of popular Democratic Governor Ted Strickland. In his time in the legislature, he was active in passing legislation to fight predatory lending which led Governor Strickland to create a Foreclosure Task Force.

OHIO'S 2ND DISTRICT

Victoria Wulsin

When we look back at Bush-Cheney and the Iraq war's biggest congressional cheerleaders humiliating themselves in Congress, "Mean Jean" Schmidt's November 2005 cheap shot on Rep. Jack Murtha ranks near the top of the list. It occurred after Murtha, who originally supported the war, realized that it was a huge mistake and supported legislation that would bring our troops home. During a debate in Congress, Mean Jean, allegedly quoting a veteran she had recently spoken to, said on the House floor,

"He asked me to send Congress a message: Stay the course. He also asked me to send Congressman Murtha a message, that cowards cut and run, Marines never do." Even though she mentioned Murtha, who served in the Marine Corps for 37 years, and she was quoting another marine, she claims she wasn't addressing anyone in particular.

She's voted with Republicans 94 percent of the time in Congress. She voted against lowering the interest rate on student loans (even 124 of her Republican colleagues supported this one, along with the Democrats).

Democratic candidate *Victoria Wulsin* challenged Mean Jean in 2006 and came within 3,000 votes of defeating her. This is supposed to be a conservative Republican district, but the Republicans have an unpopular candidate who Wulsin almost defeated before, and she should put up a good fight again. She is a doctor and a mother and has won more Democratic votes in the district than anyone before her. Dr. Wulsin has taken the pledge that all members of Congress and congressional candidates should take: "I have pledged not to take taxpayer-funded insurance until all Americans have access to quality, affordable care." She also pledged to not take any contributions from the pharmaceutical industry. She is also calling for a quick end to the war in Iraq and says, "It's unfair that well-connected defense contractors like Blackwater and Halliburton get special no-bid contracts without any accountability."

OHIO'S 16TH DISTRICT

Despite being anointed by the retiring Rep. Regula, who held this seat since the 1950s, Republicans are not high on fellow GOP-member Kirk Schuring. A State Senator who formerly served in the Ohio House of

John Boccieri

Representatives, Schuring successfully sponsored a bill that overturned a predatory lending statute in Cleveland, a fateful move that contributed to the financial struggles of many of Cleveland's formerly middle-class neighborhoods.

A Major in the Air Force Reserve, Democratic candidate *John Boccieri* served in both Iraq and Afghanistan and more than 40 countries during his 13 years in the U.S. military. He's also held political office in Ohio as both a State Representative and State Senator, where he's worked on veterans' issues, including sponsoring the Military Injury Relief Fund to help Ohio vets transition to civilian life and afford their medical bills. He's been endorsed by VoteVets.org and Progressive Patriots.

PENNSYLVANIA'S 6TH DISTRICT

Bob Roggio

Republican Jim Gerlach has won 3 elections in a row by 3 percentage points or less, so the Democrats hope they can finally get over the top in 2008. He, too, has received campaign funds from Tom DeLay's political action committee and has also been fined by the Federal Election Commission for campaign finance violations. He's actually pretty moderate as far as Republicans go, but one thing really sticks out in my mind: In 2005, *The Washington Post* reported on how the GOP House leadership held a "five-minute vote open for 45 minutes" in order to convince moderate Republicans in opposition to an energy bill.

The bill was titled The GAS Act, and it had the backing of the energy industry; according to the *Post,* "it was fervently opposed by environmentalists and their Democratic and Republican allies" because it provided subsidies for refiners and opened some federal land up for new refineries. Gerlach was one of those moderate Republicans who switched his vote under pressure from Tom DeLay and the Republican leadership. After 39 minutes of standing his ground, he caved. Don't we need leaders who can hold their ground for longer than that?

Democratic candidate *Bob Roggio* is a businessman who says that his opponent has been a rubber stamp for the Bush administration on Iraq, the economy, and environment. On Iraq, he says, "The war in Iraq was a mistake. Over the past 6 years, almost 4,000 brave troops have been killed, and close to 20,000 more injured (the number is actually over 70,000). We have spent hundreds of billions of dollars, while ignoring the very real domestic needs of our country. President Bush continues to ask for more money, and more troops, but has no new ideas to win the peace. I will fight to end this war, and bring our troops home responsibly, and with honor."

VIRGINIA'S 11TH DISTRICT

Gerald Connolly

Keith Fimian is trying to hold on to Rep. Tom Davis' seat for the Republicans, but Virginia is turning blue, and Fimian, a wealthy conservative, faces an uphill battle. Although he has the backing of the Republican whose seat he is trying to fill, the strongest praise Tom Davis gave to Fimian in a recent interview with the *Washington Post* was that he's a "credible candidate," and "He's much better-looking than I am."

A member of the Fairfax County Board of Supervisors, Democratic challenger *Gerald Connolly* could be a real leader in Congress on the environment. Most candidates call themselves "pro-environment" whether or not they've done something about it or have any serious plans to do something about it; Connolly has both. He worked with the Sierra Club on the "Cool Counties" initiative to fight global warming and has been part of Fairfax County's nationally recognized environmental programs on parkland preservation, green building policies, and watershed restoration. He is serious about his environmental agenda for Congress and has a detailed plan that you can see by visiting www.gerryconnolly.com/Environment.

He was also against the Iraq war from the beginning.

WASHINGTON'S 8TH DISTRICT

Darcy Burner

Name a notorious figure in the Republican Party and you'll probably be naming someone who's raised funds or campaigned for incumbent Dave Reichert. From George W. Bush, who made a visit to Reichert's district for a fundraiser, to former House Speaker Newt Gingrich, Dave Reichert has a long list of questionable friends. He's also received campaign money from the political action committees of two Republicans the law has already caught up with, Tom DeLay and Randy "Duke" Cunningham. Finally, he was backed by a well-known, local GOP activist named Larry Corrigan, who was arrested in an Internet sex sting for trying to arrange a sexual encounter with a 13-year-old girl. Dave needs to find some new friends.

He's voted with his fellow Republicans 84

percent of the time. This includes voting against the withdrawal of troops from Iraq, in favor of war funding with no strings attached and in favor of the FISA domestic spying legislation. Reichert is anti-abortion, opposes using federal money for sex education, and says that he supports a constitutional amendment to ban gay marriage. Back when the Republicans were in the majority in 2005, Reichert supported a bill to protect gun makers from lawsuits. It was the NRA's top legislative priority and when the bill passed it was so far reaching that it retroactively barred lawsuits against gun makers who behaved negligently and caused damage.

Democratic candidate *Darcy Burner* was raised in a blue-collar military family and vividly recalls her parents' struggle to pay off her younger sister's medical bills. After working her way up the ladder at Microsoft, she left the company in 2006 to challenge Dave Reichert, losing in a close contest. Fighting to end the Iraq war is a priority to this mother and community leader, and she also brings innovative technical expertise from one of the most high-tech districts in the country.

Darcy is typical of so many Democrats who are running this year. These 30 seats may be the most likely to win, but that's not to say another 30 can't also be won. And if that happens, we'll have a veto-proof House (should the unthinkable happen).

Ultimately, whether this comes to be is up to you. If you live in any of these districts, volunteer as much time as you can to the campaign. If you don't live near any of them, how 'bout a road trip and spending a week or two to help out? And I know many of you could write a check to any of these candidates. Or go online and make a contribution.

Victory is close, and so is four more years of the same insanity. We have no choice. It's time to act.

Appendix

Fox News/Talk Radio/McCain Campaign Easy Guide for Lifting Lines Out of Context from This Book

Over the years, I have had to witness a silly parade of right wing talk radio hosts, Fox News commentators, and Republican Party spokespeople make up stuff about me or what I've said in the hopes that fewer people would give credence to what I have to say. It's been a losing battle for them, as I remain blessed with millions of readers and filmgoers, people who have appreciated my work and hopefully been entertained and enlightened by what they have seen. Of course, the more people buy my books or come to my movies, the more the other side ramps up the hate machine against my work. I feel sorry for them, mostly for why they are afraid to debate me on the *issues*. Instead they go after me, the person.

233

But truth is not the commerce of talk radio and Fox News and the Republican Party. In order to denigrate me, they will pull lines or statements from this book out of context, hoping to heighten the rage of their listeners and viewers against me. But this is not a good year for the Right, and I guess I've started to feel sorry for them. They will be out of power soon, and we all know how that feels.

So, in order to make their job a bit easier, I have gone ahead and saved them the trouble by doing their work for them. Below, I have taken a number of quotes from this book out of context in the style that they are accustomed to doing. This is my gift to them on the eve of their defeat. Go ahead, Rush and Bill, Sean and Scarborough—bloviate away with any of these pre-approved, pre-taken out of context quotes from my new book. They're on me. Good luck, and enjoy your time in the desert.

p. 2–23	"The terrorists are on the run! . . . I know many of them . . . personally . . ."
p. 3	"So a million homes are snatched from hard-working Americans! THAT'S A SMALL PRICE TO PAY FOR FREEDOM!!"
p. 2	". . . the terrorists are . . . my friends . . ."
p. 3–61	". . . If you want to be free from terrorist bombings, then you have to be willing to . . . buy . . . this book . . ."
p. 3	"Unfortunately, not all soldiers in the fight against the terrorists know how to use their weapons. So we experience some fratricide. Stuff happens."

p. 8   "For me to believe . . . that Ahmadinejad guy, (he) would literally have to walk onto the stage of 'American Idol' *with the very bomb itself in his hands!* Seriously, I will have to see the actual friggin' bomb, and THEN I want him to show me that he knows how to use it."

p. 10   ". . . Iran has no nuclear program . . ."

p. 10–11   ". . . my fans in Boise . . . have WEAPONS OF MASS DESTRUCTION, TOO!"

p. 10–80   "Iran has no nuclear program or weapons of mass destruction. That's the position we should all take and not budge from until we see the mushroom cloud over . . . Jerusalem."

p. 17–18   ". . . I'd prefer that our elected representatives, instead of wearing flag pins on their lapels, . . . dropped . . . one down the bathroom sink . . ."

p. 8–26   "I will have . . . the crap kicked out of . . . Jesus himself."

p. 20   "Once, at a Fourth of July celebration, Obama stripped down to his underwear, climbed the flagpole, and screamed at the top of his lungs, 'Death to America Ferrera!'"

p. 21   "At Ronald Reagan's funeral, Obama went up to the deceased president's body and tried to tickle him."

p. 21   "On a fact-finding mission to Afghanistan, Obama mooned an entire regiment of troops."

p. 24   "I speak for that male, uneducated-but-hard-working vote!"

p. 36   "Guys going all brokeback on each other— gimme a break! The state can't sanction that."

p. 43   "Sadly, McCain's sacrifice had nothing to do with protecting the United States."

p. 36–45   ". . . In his book, *Faith of Our Fathers,* McCain wrote that he was upset that he had been limited to . . . beating up on homosexuals . . ."

p. 43–44   ". . . McCain . . . killed more than two million civilians in Vietnam (and perhaps another million in Laos and Cambodia)."

p. 45   ". . . President Nixon ordered . . . one 9/11 every single month—for 44 months."

p. 47–48   "John McCain is already using the Vietnam War in his political ads. In doing so, it makes not just what happened to *him* in Vietnam fair game for discussion, but also what he *did* to the Vietnamese."

p. 74   ". . . McCain has a good chance of winning . . ."

p. 73–74   "What a great day that was, seeing Nancy Pelosi . . . revealing the identity of a CIA agent in an act of revenge . . ."

p. 86–166   ". . . in his new book, *Mike's Election Guide,* he . . . supports drilling in ANWR. . . ."

p. 87–134   ". . . I toured the country in my own independent effort to get . . . your wife . . . inseminated . . ."

p. 86   "I just went to the same terrorist Muslim school of flag pin desecrators you went to."

APPENDIX

p. 176   "People seem to like Sen. Elizabeth Dole (R-NC). I prefer to think of it as pity. After all she's got a guy who's hooked on Viagra chasing her every night . . . with four-hour erections wanting some immediate attention."

Notes and Sources

1. "ASK MIKE!"

The information on credit card industry profits in 2003 and 2007 is from *Time Magazine,* "Exposing the Credit Card Fine Print," Anita Hamilton, February 21, 2008; it can be accessed online at *www.time.com/time/ magazine/article/0,9171,1715293,00.html.* The forecast on the number of home foreclosures in 2008 is from *USA TODAY,* "Foreclosures to have 'profound' impact, report warns," Sue Kirchhoff, November 29, 2007; *www.usatoday .com/money/economy/housing/2007-11-27-foreclosures-N.htm;* information on bankruptcy rates is from *The American Prospect* online, "A Nation Running on Empty," Elizabeth Henderson, June 6, 2007; *www.prospect.org/cs/articles? article=a_nation_running_on_empty.* published June 6, 2007. The source for the number of people with poor credit scores is Direct Lending Solutions, "2005 Consumer Statistics," Sharon Secor, accessed June 11, 2008; *www .directlendingsolutions.com/2005_consumer_stats.htm.*

For the fashion-conscious patriots among my readership, magnetic "Support Our Troops" ribbons come in red, white, and blue and camouflage in addition to the more traditional yellow. According to Rob Walker in "The Magnet Magnet," (*The New York Times Magazine,* November 7, 2004), the magnetic ribbons were apparently first produced in rural North Carolina beginning in 2003. The story goes that Dwain Gullion, a Christian bookstore owner, heard that there was a shortage of real, live, yellow ribbon to tie around trees, fence poles, and dogs' necks, and so he decided to fill the perceived need with magnetic yellow ribbons. It didn't take long, however, for others to seize upon the idea and produce their own magnetic yellow stickers, including, according to Guillon, "knockoffs made more cheaply overseas." Since Gullion focuses on selling his magnets to organizations as a fundraising effort, you can bet that any magnet you find at Wal-Mart is produced in China or somewhere else overseas.

The *Boston Globe* reported on the backlog of disabilities claims the Department of Veterans Affairs is facing in "Backlogs in disability claims seen stretching Veterans Affairs to Limit," Hope Yen, March 14, 2007. According to the article the Government Accounting Office studied the VA claims system and found it "on the verge of crisis due to backlogs, cumbersome paperwork, and ballooning costs." The study estimated that the VA will see 400,000 first-time claims due to the Iraq war by the end of 2009, costing anywhere from $70 billion to $150 billion. The article is available online at *www.boston.com/news/nation/washington/articles/2007/03/14/backlogs_in_disability_claims_seen_stretching_veterans_affairs_to_limit/.*

As of July 3, 2008, there were 4,116 U.S. military casualties from Operation Iraqi Freedom. Casualty information is from the Department of Defense Casualty Report available online at *www.defenselink.mil/news/casualty.pdf*.

In October 2001, President George W. Bush held a prime time news conference in the East Room of the White House on the state of the war on terror. During the speech the President said, "Now, the American people have got to go about their business. We cannot let the terrorists achieve the objective of frightening our nation to the point where we don't—where we don't conduct business, where people don't shop." A transcript of the complete speech is available online at *www.whitehouse.gov/news/releases/2001/10/20011011-7.html*.

The Center for Public Integrity's War Card website is an excellent resource for the many lies told by the Bush Administration leading up to the Iraq war. Check it out at *www.publicintegrity.org/WarCard*. In particular, see the "Key False Statements" section.

The first Scott McClellan quote is from pp. 156–157 of his 2008 memoir, *What Happened: Inside the Bush White House and Washington's Culture of Deception* (Public Affairs, 2008). The second quote is from *Countdown with Keith Olbermann*, Thursday, May 29, 2008; *www.msnbc.msn.com/id/24893045/*.

Leading up to the 2004 election between John Kerry and George W. Bush, a Zogby/Williams Identity Poll reported that 57 percent of undecided voters would rather have a beer with Bush than Kerry. For more on candidates and beer, see *The Hill*, "Drink Up," Betsy Rothstein, June 25, 2008; *http://thehill.com/cover-stories/drink-up-2008-06-25.html*.

The lyrics to "I've Got a Crush on Obama" are reprinted with permission of Ben Relles, creator of BarelyPolitical .com, a political satire website that Relles launched in June 2007 with the viral video "I Got a Crush on Obama," featuring Obama Girl. In its first year BarelyPolitical videos were seen over 100 million times online and featured on programs including the BBC, ABC, NBC, CNN and Fox News.

ABC news is the source for Barack Obama's quote regarding the absence of a flag pin on his lapel. The story was reported in "Obama Dropped Flag Pin in War Statement," David Wright and Sunlen Miller, October 4, 2007; *http://abcnews.go.com/Politics/story?id=3690000&page=1.*

The quote on the Catholic Church's position on contraception is from *Vade Mecum for Confessors Concerning Some Aspects of the Morality of Conjugal Life* issued by the Vatican's Pontifical Council for the Family on March 1, 1997; *www.vatican.va/roman_curia/pontifical_councils/family/ documents/rc_pc_family_doc_12021997_vademecum_en .html.*

In 2001 the National Conference of Catholic Bishops voted 209 to 7 to declare sterilization "intrinsically evil," condemning tubal ligation and vasectomies and putting them on equal footing with abortion and euthanasia. Here's the quote from "Ethical and Religious Directives for Catholic Health Care Services, Fourth Edition," June 15, 2001; *www.usccb.org/bishops/directives.shtml*:

> While there are many acts of varying moral gravity that can be identified as intrinsically evil, in the context of contemporary health care the most pressing

concerns are currently abortion, euthanasia, assisted suicide, and direct sterilization.

The gang of Catholic bishops struck again on June 13, 2008, at their conference in Orlando, Florida, when they voted 191–1 to adopt a statement condemning embryonic stem cell research, as reported by Reuters, "Bishops condemn stem cell research," Barbara Liston, June 13, 2008; *www.reuters.com/article/healthNews/idUSN131220080613*.

The Pew Research Center survey on Catholics' position on social issues is from August 2007. It can be found online at *http://pewresearch.org/pubs/778/a-portrait-of-american-catholics-on-the-eve-of-pope-benedicts-visit*. In addition, a 2005 survey by CNN/USA Today/Gallup found that 78% of Catholics believed the pope should allow Catholics to use birth control; 63% were in favor of letting priests marry; 59% wanted a less-strict policy on stem cell research. CNN.com, "Poll: U.S. Catholics Would Support Changes," *www.cnn.com/2005/US/04/03/pope .poll/index.html*.

According to *The Boston Globe,* the United States Catholic bishops estimate that 96 percent of married Catholics use birth control; "Bishops Stress Sexual Issues and Warn on Communion," Michael Paulson, November 15, 2006; *www.boston.com/news/nation/articles/2006/11/15/bishops_stress_sexual_issues_and_warn_on_communion*.

Regarding the legal status and voting rights of women at the time this country was founded, see "The Legal Status of Women, 1776–1830," Marylynn Salmon, *www.historynow.org/03_2006/historian3.html*. Salmon says that "Women, no matter how wealthy, did not have the right to vote, even though women paid the same taxes as men. The reasoning behind this discrimination rested on the assumption that "married women were liable to coercion by their husbands; if a wife voted, legislators argued, it meant that a man cast two ballots." Salmon also points out that, "By marriage, the very being or legal existence of the woman was suspended during the marriage, or at least was incorporated into that of the husband: under whose wing, protection, and cover, she performed every thing." A husband and wife could sign a contract called a "marriage settlement" that enabled the woman to own property separately from her husband; however, such contracts were rare and illegal in some areas.

Women's Suffrage Amendments were introduced in the United States Congress in 1878 and 1914, but failed to pass. The wording of the 1878 amendment was the same as the Nineteenth Amendment, which passed both houses of Congress in 1919 and was ratified on August 26, 1920. Here's the wording of the amendment:

> The right of citizens of the United States to vote shall not be denied or abridged by the United States or by any State on account of sex. Congress shall have power to enforce this article by appropriate legislation.

Only 1 of the 68 women who signed the Declaration of Sentiments at Seneca Falls in 1848 lived to see women be given the right to vote in 1920. But according to historian Judith Wellman, 92-year-old Charlotte Woodward

Pierce probably never actually cast a vote, as she was sick on election day in 1920.

The sources for Sen. Thad Cochran's comments about McCain's temper are *The Boston Globe,* "Famed McCain temper is tamed," Kranish, Michael, January 7, 2008; *www.boston.com/news/nation/articles/2008/01/27/famed_mccain_temper_is_tamed/*; *Biloxi Sun Herald,* "Cochran recounts McCain dustup with the Sandinistas," Michael Newsom, July 1, 2008; *www.sunherald.com/newsupdates/story/660742.html*; Politico.com, "Thad Cochran not helping the cause," Jonathan Martin, July 2, 2008; *www.politico.com/blogs/jonathanmartin/0708/Thad_Cochran_not_helping_the_cause.html*. Sen. Bob Smith's comments are from the same Jonathan Martin article. Other quotes are from *Free Ride: John McCain and the Media,* David Brock and Paul Waldman, Anchor Books, 2008; and *The Real McCain,* Cliff Schecter, PoliPoint Press, 2008.

Vietnamese civilian casualty numbers are from the Vietnamese Government's official casualty report, released in April 1995 and reported by the Associated Press, "The End of a War, Death of a Nation Remembered 20 Years Later," George Esper, April 9, 1995. Other sources for Vietnam War statistics include the *The Boston Globe,* "The Christmas Bombings," James Carroll, December 24, 2002; reprinted on the CommonDreams.org website *www.commondreams.org/views02/1224–04.htm*; *Setup: What the Air Force Did in Vietnam and Why,* Earl H. Tilford, Maxwell Air Force Base, AL: Air University Press, 1991; *Like Rolling Thunder: The Air War in Vietnam, 1964–1975,* Ronald Bruce Frankum, Rowman & Littlefield, 2005; *A History of Modern Wars of Attrition,* Carter

Malkasian, Greenwood Publishing Group, 2002; *The Vietnam War: Vietnamese and American Perspectives,* Mark Bradley, et al., M.E. Sharpe, 1993; *What Should We Tell Our Children About Vietnam?* Bill McCloud, U. of Oklahoma Press, 2000; *Bombing to Win: Air Power and Coercion in War,* Robert Pape, Cornell University Press, 1996; *Strategic Terror: The Politics and Ethics of Aerial Bombardment,* Beau Grosscup, Zed Books, 2006.

Information on the U.S. Electoral College is from the National Archives website in a section devoted to the U.S. Electoral College (*www.archives.gov/federal-register/electoral-college*). Regarding the process for selecting electors, according to the Archives it's generally the case that "the political parties nominate electors at their State party conventions or by a vote of the party's central committee in each State. Electors are often selected to recognize their service and dedication to their political party. They may be State elected officials, party leaders, or persons who have a personal or political affiliation with the Presidential candidate." Further, the Archives state that there is no Constitutional or Federal provision requiring electors to adhere to the results of the popular vote in their state. However, 26 states and the District of Columbia have state laws binding electors to cast their vote for a specific candidate.

The information on the crazy cool democracy in ancient Greece comes from Professor Paul Cartledge's article "The Democratic Experiment" on the BBC website on Ancient Greek History at *http://www.bbc.co.uk/history/ancient/greeks/greekdemocracy_01.shtml.*

The Center for Responsive Politics collects data on re-election rates and reported that between 1998 and 2006 congressional incumbents were reelected an average of 96.8 percent of the time. The lowest re-election rate in the past 30 years was 88 percent in 1992. Detailed information is available online at *www.opensecrets.org/bigpicture/reelect.php?cycle=2006*. Senate re-election rates are slightly lower, at 79 percent in 2000 and 2006, 96 percent in 2004, and 86 percent in 2002.

The Center for Responsive Politics tracks the amount of money various business sectors and lobbying organizations contribute to presidential campaigns. Check out their website at *www.opensecrets.org*. The amounts listed were as of May 21, 2008.

Information on the amount of money that gun rights and gun control advocates have contributed to presidential campaigns is from the Center for Responsive Politics' Issue Profile, "Gun Control vs. Gun Rights." It is available online at *http://opensecrets.org/news/issues/guns/index.php*.

Former Senator Phil Gramm's connection to the McCain campaign and his efforts to deregulate the banking industry is detailed by MSNBC.com, "McCain Economic Policy Shaped by Lobbyist," Jonathan Larsen and Keith Olbermann, March 28, 2008; *www.msnbc.msn.com/id/24844889/*.

One good source for information about John McCain and how the press has covered him they way they covered candidate Bush is *Free Ride: John McCain and the Media*, David Brock and Paul Waldman, Anchor Books, 2008. See pages 49 to 58.

For an excellent discussion of why the Democrats should forget about the South and instead concentrate on the Mountain West and shoring up support in traditionally blue states, see *Whistling Past Dixie: How Democrats Can Win Without the South,* Thomas F. Schaller (New York: Simon & Schuster, 2006; with a new Afterword in 2008).

The Union of Concerned Scientists "World Wide Nuclear Arsenals" fact sheet, July 2007, reports that the United States has 10,000 nuclear warheads and Russia has 15,000. Together, these two countries have more than 96 percent of the world's total nuclear arsenal. The information can be accessed online at *www.ucsusa .org/global_security/nuclear_weapons/worldwide-nuclear-arsenals.html.*

Little League Baseball changed its rules for pitches in all divisions beginning with the 2007 season. The pitch limit varies by age, and the more pitches a player throws the longer he must rest before pitching again. For complete rules see "Little League Implements New Rule to Protect Pitchers' Arms," published on August 25, 2006, and posted on the site *www.littleleague.org/media/pitch_ count_08–25–06.asp.*

2. HOW TO ELECT JOHN MCCAIN

A full transcript of Barack Obama's June 4, 2008, speech before the American Israel Public Affairs Committee is available from National Public Radio, "Transcript: Obama's Speech at AIPAC," June 4, 2008; *www.npr.org/templates/ story/story.php?storyId=91150432.*

For a full transcript of John Kerry's denial of having seen *Fahrenheit 9/11,* go to *http://transcripts.cnn.com/ TRANSCRIPTS/0407/08/lkl.00.html.* The interview aired on CNN's *Larry King Live* on July 8, 2004.

3. TEN PRESIDENTIAL DECREES FOR HIS
FIRST TEN DAYS

Don't believe me that government-run healthcare systems cost less and provide better care than our screwed up market-based system? Then maybe you will believe the Organisation for Economic Co-operation and Development. Its *OECD Health Data 2007,* published in July 2007 (*http://miranda.sourceoecd.org/vl=2536797/cl=15/nw=1/ rpsv/figures_2007/en/page2.htm*), reported on the health spending and resources for all member countries, including Canada, France, Sweden, the United Kingdom, and the United States. The U.S. spends 15.3 percent of its GDP on health care, as opposed to Canada (9.8%), France (11.1%), Sweden (9.1%), and the United Kingdom (8.3%). No OECD member country spends a larger percentage of their GDP on healthcare than the United States.

The World Health Organization, "World Health Statistics 2008—Mortality and Burden of Disease," tracks the life expectancy at birth for countries around the world. The life expectancy for someone living in the United States is 78, compared to 79 in the United Kingdom, and 81 in Canada, France, and Sweden. See pp. 36–44 of *www.who.int/whosis/whostat/2008/en/index.html.*

The Library of Congress reports that HR 676 has 90 co-sponsors: *http://thomas.loc.gov/cgi-bin/bdquery/z?d110: h.r.00676.* For more information on John Conyer's HR 676, United States National Health Insurance Act, go to *www.pnhp.org/publications/the_national_health_insurance_ bill_hr_676.php*, a site run by Physicians for a National Health Program.

For information on who pays for drug research, see the following sources: *The Truth About Drug Companies,* Marcia Angell, Random House: New York, 2004; *New York Times,* "Drug Companies Profit From Research Supported by Taxpayers," Jeff Gerth and Sheryl Gay Stolberg, April 23, 2000; *www.nytimes.com/library/national/science/health/042300hth-drugs2.html; Frontline: The Other Drug War,* Interview with Marcia Angell, PBS.com: *www.pbs.org/wgbh/pages/frontline/shows/other/interviews/angell.html.* Marcia Angell is quoted on *Frontline* as saying:

> The pharmaceutical industry likes to depict itself as a research-based industry, as the source of innovative drugs. Nothing could be further from the truth. This is their incredible PR and their nerve.
>
> In fact, if you look at where the original research comes from on which new drugs are based, it tends to be from the NIH [National Institutes of Health], from the academic medical centers, and from foreign academic medical centers. Studies of this, looking at the seminal research on which drug patents are based, have found that about 15 percent of the basic research papers, reporting the basic research, came from industry. That's just 15 percent.
>
> The other 85 percent came from NIH-supported work carried out in American academic medical centers. In one study, 30 percent came from foreign academic medical centers. So what we know about the numbers indicates that the foreign academic medical centers are responsible for more new drug discoveries than the industry itself.

All tax data for comparing French and American taxes is from "OECD Taxing Wages Statistics 2007." The figures cited are for a two-earner married couple, one at 100 percent of average earnings and the other at 67 percent of average earnings, with two children. The figures are based on total tax payments less cash transfers, which the OECD defines as "employees' social security contributions and personal income tax less transfer payments as a percentage of gross wage earnings." Without taking cash transfers into account, the tax rate is higher for French families with children, but because the government transfers money back to the families, subtracting the amount of the cash transfer from the total tax bill is a more accurate reflection of actual costs.

According to the French Embassy in Washington, DC, the French social security code puts no limitation on the number of allowable paid sick days per year, except in the case of long-term illness, which is generally considered to be between 1 and 2 months. In that case, the employer does have the right to begin taking steps to lay a person off. At that point the social security system picks up the bill and supports the ill person.

My primary source for material on the history of high fructose corn syrup is Greg Critzer's *Fat Land: How Americans Became the Fattest People in the World* (Boston: Houghton Mifflin Co, 2003), which should be required reading in all high schools. Additional sources on HFCS include www.grist.org, "ADM, high-fructose corn syrup, and ethanol," Tom Philpott, May 10, 2006, *http://gristmill .grist.org/story/2006/5/10/135951/485*; *New York Times*, "Seeing Sugar's Future in Fuel," Clifford Kraus, October 18,

2007, *www.nytimes.com/2007/10/18/business/18sugar.html? pagewanted=1&—r=1*; *New York Times Magazine,* "The (Agri)Cultural Contradictions of Obesity," Michael Pollan, October 12, 2003, *http://www.michaelpollan.com/article .php?id=52*; and www.cato.org, "Archer Daniels Midland: A Case Study in Corporate Welfare, James Bovard, September 26, 1995, *www.cato.org/pubs/pas/pa-241.html.* For additional information on the number of people without clean drinking water or basic sewer systems, see WHO, "Drinking Water, Sanitation, Health and Disease," *www.who.int/water_sanitation_health/mdg1/en/index.html.* Although it is certainly the case that the cost of digging a well in a third world country varies greatly depending on the type of well and numerous other factors, according to sources at Africare and the Millennium Water Alliance, $10 per person is a conservative estimate.

Information on the Social Security tax ceiling and keeping the trust funds solvent by eliminating the ceiling was obtained from the Congressional Research Service report by Debra Whitman titled "Social Security: Raising or Eliminating the Taxable Earnings Base," Congressional Research Service-CRS Report for Congress, January 26, 2006; *http://assets.opencrs.com/rpts/RL32896_20060126 .pdf.* It states, "If all earnings were subject to the payroll tax but the base was retained for benefit calculations, the Social Security Trust Funds would remain solvent for the next 75 years . . ."

In 1982 the percent of covered earnings that were taxed for Social Security was 90 percent; in 2004 that number was down to 85 percent. That percentage is projected to fall to 83 percent for 2014 and later.

According to the 2006 Congressional Report on Congress, "if the base was completely eliminated for both employers and employees so that all earnings were taxed, but those earnings did not count toward benefits, solvency would be restored to Social Security. The increased revenue would eliminate 116% of the projected shortfall and the program would have surplus of 0.32% of wages. Under this scenario, the payroll tax rate could be immediately *lowered* by 2.6% of taxable payroll (from 12.4% to 9.8%), and the system would remain solvent for the next 75 years. However, the traditional link between the level of wages that are taxed and the level of wages that count toward benefits would be broken."

Source material for the history of the Pledge of Allegiance and Francis Bellamy is from "What's Conservative about the Pledge of Allegiance?" by Gene Healy, www.cato.org, November 4, 2003; "The History of the Pledge of Allegiance," Associated Press, June 14, 2004; and *Washington Post*, "The Pledge of Allegiance; The Big Story—An Occasional Look at What Everyone Is Talking About," May 23, 2004.

4. Six Modest Proposals to Fix Our Broken Elections

The *New York Times Magazine* reported on the estimated failure rate of electronic voting machines in "Can You Count on Voting Machines?" by Clive Thompson, January 6, 2008, *www.nytimes.com/2008/01/06/magazine/06Vote-t.html*.

The source for information on voter turnout is International Institute for Democracy and Electoral Assistance,

"Voter Turnout Rates from a Comparative Perspective," Rafael López Pintor, Maria Gratschew and Kate Sullivan, *www.idea.int/publications/vt/upload/Voter%20turnout.pdf* (see page 80 for U.S. in comparison to Western Europe and North America).

Voting machine failure rates are from the *Los Angeles Times,* "Tallying the Woes of Electronic Balloting," Chris Gaither, September 24, 2004, and accessed online at *www.votersunite.org/article.asp?id=2907*.

Obama's fundraising information is from the Campaign Finance Institute, "Newly Released 2007 Reports Give Clues to Candidates' Financial Strengths and Vulnerabilities Going into Super Tuesday," February 1, 2008; *www.cfinst.org/pr/prRelease.aspx?ReleaseID=177*.

For information on why we vote on Tuesdays, see S. 2638: Weekend Voting Act, GovTrack.US; *www.govtrack.us/congress/bill.xpd?bill=s110–2638*.

For info on Canada's "National Register of Electors" and how they used to have a U.S.-like inefficient voter registration process, visit the official Canadian Election website: www.elections.ca.

Acknowledgments

Thanks to my publisher, Grand Central Publishing, for the unconditional support and commitment to get this book in the hands of as many voters as possible. Grand Central used to be called Warner Books and was part of the TimeWarner empire. Then the French bought Warner Books, so I guess you could say I now work for the French. One more talking point for O'Reilly.

My special thanks to my personal publisher and editor there, Jamie Raab, who is a dream come true—every writer should be so lucky. Thanks also to the great staff at Grand Central: managing editor Bob Castillo, Anne Twomey, Anna Maria Piluso, Toni Marotta, Jimmy Franco, Martha Otis, Chris Barba, Bruce Paonessa, and

the rest of the Hachette Book Group sales force—
merci beaucoup! They all let me write right up until the presses ran so that this guide could be as
current as possible. Special thanks to the chair of
Hachette USA, David Young.

Thanks to my agent and the Deep Throat of
my world, Mort Janklow. He knows where the
bodies are buried. And to the wonderful Anne
Sibbald at Janklow, Nesbit. Someday I hope to
meet Nesbit.

Thanks to Basel Hamdan, Cory Fisher, Eric
Weinrib, and Jennifer Moore for all their help in re-
searching and working on this book. Thanks to
Christine Fall, Curt Webb, and John Raths for
photographing the people on the street. Thanks to
Jenn Craven for assisting me during this process.

The cover of this book was designed by Tom
Kluepful at Doyle Partners.

Thanks to Al Hirvela for suggesting the idea for
Chapter Two and to Rod Birleson for numerous
discussions about everything else. Thanks also
to them and Joanne Doroshow, Ann Cohen, Jeff
Gibbs, Fred and Jackie Trimble, Shirley Williams,
and Deborah Lake for reading the draft and for
their helpful comments. Their unhelpful ones
were useful, too.

Special thanks to my sisters Anne and Veronica for their feedback and encouragement. Thanks also to my bros-in-law John and Rocky for reading the final draft and for their support.

This book was written in downtown Traverse City, Michigan. Come visit the historic State Theatre art house if you're ever in the area. It shows only the best movies, the picture and sound are perfect, and the pop and popcorn can be had for $2. We put on a film festival here every end of July in the hopes of saving it and supporting the art of cinema. Thanks to all the people here who have made this a nice place to think and create.

And thanks to all of you who continue to read my books and go to my movies. Though I sadly don't have the time to answer most of my mail, I do read it and am eternally grateful for your kind words and your own commitment to making a better world. Don't give up, we're all in this together.

Finally, thanks to Kathleen and Natalie. And Lily, northern Michigan's Dog of the Year. She got over her disappointment in Hillary's narrow loss and is now working hard for Obama.